RECENT READER

"Better than a 'how to' parenting guide,
we learned)' guide for domestic and international travel. Practical, positive, and realistic, the zest to see the world and open that world up to one's child is contagious, at least it was to this reader. 'Bravo!'"
— Carl Pickhardt Ph.D, author of: WHO STOLE MY CHILD—parenting through four stages of adolescence

"I have bought and read your book. It's amazing! I love your approach to travel and have found lots of new tips, strategies and advice. You have done a great job of creating this book!" — Kateryna, Mom

"Whether you're taking a weekend road trip, or a month-long European vacation, there is useful advice in this book. They've thought of everything from packing efficiently with enough snacks to how to board a train with a stroller. I especially appreciated some of the pro tips for long-distance travel. Their seat hacking strategy for airlines is perfect ..." — Aaron, Dad

"I loved this book! It has great ideas for how to manage traveling with kids (domestically and internationally)! I love the packing checklist and educational app suggestions to keep kids busy on flights!" — Abby, Mom

"The tips and tricks presented by the authors are very helpful when traveling with young kids. I have 3 young daughters; and travelling always used to be a challenge. After reading this book "How To Travel With Kids", I have gained new insights and travel tips that I normally would not have thought off. Kudos to the authors; I would highly recommend this book to any families who love to travel with their kids!" — Hussein, Dad

"This book is informative, relatable, down to earth, & fun to read. Adventurous couple! Great tips to cut down your stress on traveling with a toddler/kid. I bought some assorted packing cubes on Amazon. ;-) Great tip!" — Terri, Mom

"The book is full of tips and advice that I would have never thought of it by myself. MUST READ for anyone who dreams about traveling and is worried about traveling with kids. I appreciate how AJ and Natasha provided tips and best practices on planning, packing, using technology, etc. For me, it also served as an inspiration to travel. Well done!" — Manny, Dad

"We have a 7 year old and 3 year old—this book helped us prepare for a 2 week long trip to Maine including how to pack and what to bring. We haven't tried AirBnB with our kids yet but that's a great tip! If you're planning a trip of more than a few nights with kids—this book will save you a lot of heartaches." — Samantha, Mom

"After having a child, I was constantly concerned about being "those people" on the plane or hotel or restaurant, but the tips found in "How to Travel with Kids" have made traveling with our daughter so much easier. This book allowed us to stop postponing travel or fretting about long flights and made it easy for us to embrace traveling as a family of three. We are able to share the world and new experiences with her, and a big reason is because of this book!" — David, Dad

"This book covers all that you'll need for a successful and fun family trip. Simple to read with great tips coming from real experience, including ideas that would have never crossed my mind. The product recommendations are so helpful ..." — Laura, Mom

How to Travel
WITH KIDS
WITHOUT LOSING YOUR MIND

Real World Tips and Practical Solutions For Traveling With Your Children

How to Travel
WITH KIDS
WITHOUT LOSING YOUR MIND

Real World Tips and Practical Solutions For Traveling With Your Children

NATASHA SANDHIR & AJ RATANI

Dedicated to our loving parents who gave us opportunities that led to this wonderful journey.

"To travel is to live."

- Hans Christian Andersen

Table of Contents

Meet The 2 Idiots

Beginning in the summer of 2017, we embarked upon a journey together—a big one spanning 31 countries, and comprising of 40 flights, 3 cruises, and 100+ destinations. But we are getting ahead of ourselves—let us tell you how this all got started!

For years, we had entertained the idea of taking an extended trip around the world with our son, Aarav. We thought about waiting until he was older, until we were more established, until everything. **Then we decided, let's just do it. Now!**

CARRYING AARAV LIKE A KING IN THE FORBIDDEN CITY IN BEIJING, CHINA

We planned and strategized, and *then* we told our family and friends our plans. Their response?

"What are you guys, idiots?"

Why yes, we are! We are The 2 Idiots and a toddler exploring the world. We travel by air, land, and sea. Travel is our passion, and globetrotting with our child is our lifestyle. Our goal is to help parents realize that traveling with kids is not as bad as it seems. We hope our journey will inspire you as you plan your own adventures!

The world can be your oyster—even if you have kids! We are so happy that you have purchased our book, so let us take a moment to introduce ourselves.

AJ's story

After spending several years climbing the corporate ladder, I made the decision to leave my high-profile position at a fast-growing company to embark upon a new road in my career. First though, I wanted to take a sabbatical to clear my head and spend some time with my wife Natasha and our son Aarav. A passionate traveler my entire life, I had been entertaining the thought for a few years of taking an extended trip around the world, and after consulting extensively with Natasha, the two of us decided to make this fantasy a reality.

Natasha's story

Of course, at first I must admit that I didn't think AJ was serious about this whole idea, and I was even less sure that we could actually make it work. Let me just say that I am a reluctant world traveler; I wasn't against the idea of exploring the globe, but, if I am being honest, I simply appreciate and need structure and organization in my life. Quite frankly, I couldn't picture what spending months and months globetrotting would look like—and what it would mean for my family. However, together, we figured it out. We planned, we strategized, and we worked together until we came to the realization that it is possible to engage in both long- and short-term travel with a child in tow! We are proof that you can pursue your dreams of world travel!

What followed was an eight-and-a-half-month adventure—something we are incredibly grateful for and feel very lucky and privileged to have done. We learned a lot about ourselves, our relationship with each other, and our relationship with our son. We also acquired some valuable knowledge and skills about not only how to travel, but how to do it with a young child.

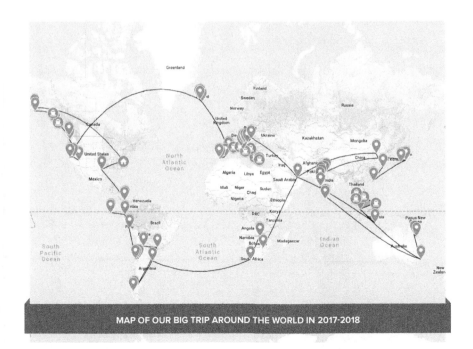

MAP OF OUR BIG TRIP AROUND THE WORLD IN 2017-2018

We hope that your own sense of wanderlust grows as you read and learn about our travels—and that, in turn, you realize you can journey throughout the world while also keeping your loved ones close by, truly seeing the world together.

Countries we visited as a family:

Argentina
Australia
Bahamas
Botswana
Cambodia
Canada
Chile
China
Croatia
Denmark
Ecuador

England
Estonia
Finland
France
Germany
Grand Cayman
Greece
Hong Kong
Hungary
Iceland
India

Indonesia
Italy
Japan
Macau
Malaysia
Montenegro
Panama
Peru
Russia
Singapore
Slovenia

South Africa
Spain
Sweden
Switzerland
Thailand
UAE
United States
Zimbabwe

Our Stats:

Age of our child: 3

Countries we visited as a family: 41

Cruises taken as a family: 4

Flights taken as a family: 73

Unique Destinations traveled as a family: 110

Total Destinations traveled as a family: 124

Guide to our book

This indicates a personal story from our travels that we want to share.

 This indicates an external link and is an additional resource to help you in your travel journey. Visit our resources page at www.the2idiots.com/resources/ for a digital download of this book and comprehensive list of links to our referenced articles, recommended products, downloadable checklists and more.

"Travel with your kids and let them surprise you."

This indicates a tip we think is particularly important. You will see a lot of these throughout the book.

Be F.L.E.X.I.

Our Travel Philosophy:
Be F.L.E.X.I.B.L.E.

We didn't want to stop seeing the world after we had a child. Rather, we wanted to experience the world *with* our son. And after traveling the world as a family, we learned that flexibility is the key to a successful trip. This has now become our travel mantra, and we will show you how to implement it throughout this book.

Here is what we mean to **Be F.L.E.X.I.B.L.E.**:

Focus: Focus on your child, not others.

How many times have you boarded on a plane and got the "oh, no, they have a toddler" look? This is your life and your family; learn how to focus on your children and not on a stranger's judgment.

Live: Live your life and don't wait for the perfect time to travel. Do it now!

Do you know that 15 percent of your adult life will be spent with your young children? You'll never get these days back so live for the here and now. There is no perfect time to travel, so why not do it now?

Empathize: Empathize with each other, with your children and with other families.

Traveling with young children is not easy and empathy is critical. Learn how we supported each other through our travels and got stronger as a family.

Xperience: Experience new things and build amazing memories!

Don't be afraid of trying things you did prior to having kids. Learn how we snorkeled in the Galapagos, went on a safari, and enjoyed many amazing excursions with Aarav. If you have been holding off on these experiences, maybe it's time to experiment!

Improvise: Improvise and go with the flow.

As parents you improvise all the time! It's exactly the same when you travel with your kids. Learn how to manage through jet-lag, fussy dinners and toddler meltdowns without losing your mind.

Be Prepared: Prepare mentally and have a plan for when things go wrong.

There are so many ways you can be prepared on your travels. Learn how to get in the right frame of mind, pack the essentials, adjust as needed and be ready when things go wrong.

Learn: Understand you won't have a perfect trip but you will learn as you go along.

Everything you do as a parent is a learning experience, and travel is no different. Every trip will get better because you will learn how to overcome obstacles the next time around.

Embrace Technology: Use technology to make your travels easier.

Technology has come a long way. Learn how to use technology to plan an amazing trip, save money, educate and entertain your child. Technology does not have to be a foe - learn to make it your friend!

There you have it: **Be F.L.E.X.I.B.L.E.** That's the foundation to each and every story and tip we offer and you'll find it throughout the book. **Make it your mantra, too.**

Why Wait? Travel Now!

So many people have told us that they are waiting to have children until after they see the world. Or they are waiting to travel until their children are older. We say, why wait? *Travel now.*

AARAV ENJOYING A PARK IN BUDAPEST

Experience now. Having young children should not keep you from going where you want to go, and they always make it more interesting.

There are countless excuses for not traveling with children, and we hear you. It can be a lot of work— but it can also be an amazing experience. There will never be a perfect time to travel with your child, so do it now before the opportunity passes you by. Don't worry so much about the *what ifs*. Instead, seize whatever opportunities come your way for travel and adventure, regardless of your child's age.

Based on "Live" from Be F.L.E.X.I.B.L.E., this chapter will encourage you to set out on an adventure with your family. Remember, there is never a perfect time to travel. Life happens, and something will always pop up that keeps you from pursuing your dreams, if you let it.

There will always be reasons not to go. We think the reasons to go are more compelling, and we hope you'll seriously consider it.

···

We go because...

Traveling is a perfect way to spend **quality time** together. We enjoyed our experiences even if they didn't go smoothly. Sometimes it's the things that went wrong that made the trip more memorable and fun anyway.

Through our travels, we have learned to become **more flexible** people. Life is always unpredictable, and that's especially true when you're on vacation. Your whole trip is a disruption to your regular routine, but you learn to roll with it. Learning that has made our marriage stronger and made us more relaxed parents.

"Travel with your kids and let them surprise you."

Traveling will expose you to **new ideas, cultures, and experiences.** Whether you are traveling across the country or around the world, you see firsthand how others live and how their cultures and routines differ from your own. This has helped our family become more **adaptable, resilient, and adventurous.**

We also discovered how welcoming people can be, especially toward little ones. All of our preconceived notions and worries vanished when we saw how supportive others were.

Possibly the most important reason to travel **is to build memories** that will outlast any gadget or toy you can buy. When we look back at our childhoods, we don't think about all the toys we had or didn't have; instead, we think about the fun experiences we had. The late-night movies. Getting pulled out of school to go for an ice cream. All the new places we got to see as we traveled with our families. **Those memories are treasures to us, and far more valuable than things.** Traveling with our son has given us memories that will last forever. The first time he said "elephant," we were in Botswana. One time we had to change a poopy diaper on a tour in Argentina. The first time he was in a helicopter, we were flying over Victoria Falls. We will show him the pictures and videos as he grows up and make more memories as we continue to travel. **We will talk about these experiences for the rest of our lives.**

ELEPHANTS IN BOTSWANA - AARAV SAID "ELEPHANT" FOR THE FIRST TIME

· ·

Fears and excuses

Some people want to travel but are afraid or don't know how. Others want to wait until their kids are older, or until they get a better job, or after they lose some weight. If it is something you truly want to do, why let fear stand in your way? We hope we can help you move past your excuses and dispel some of your fears, so you can feel confident when you travel.

1. I will wait until my kids are _____.

Why does your child have to be a certain age before you can go places and do things? We realize that we are not the norm when it comes to parenting and traveling, but we really enjoy our lifestyle. Traveling with your child depends more upon your **readiness and flexibility** as the parent than upon your child's age.

In some ways, it's almost easier to travel with kids when they are younger — they don't get easily "bored" and likely will just follow you and your plans. And you can generally create the schedule you want with them along for the ride (we think it's great to do activities with them too, and we talk about that in *How To Take Your Kids Anywhere!*).

We took Aarav on his first road trip when he was four weeks old. He had his first flight when he was four months old. We highly encourage you to take at least one trip (even a short road trip) by the time your child is **six months old**. We know it can be a little scary, but by starting sooner, you'll realize it really isn't as overwhelming as you think it will be and we hope that our book can inspire you to travel earlier than you expected!

· ·

2. Traveling with a child is expensive.

Pick a place you have always wanted to go. Research the cost. This is very simple to do. Check on flight prices, typical accommodation costs, visa/passport fees, and then decide if it really is too expensive to go. For accommodations, shop around and make sure you consider options like Airbnb (see *Our Accomodation Survival Guide* for more information) that can significantly reduce costs over staying in hotels.

For flights, you have the option to *not* purchase your child their own seat if they are under two years old—so it can actually be cheaper to travel with kids when they are younger. Also, check prices at multiple airports nearby.

If it is more than you can afford, **create a travel budget** and start saving. If the cost still seems prohibitive, see if you can travel during the off-season. This can cut the cost of your trip *significantly!*

Remember, you don't have to be rich to realize your travel dreams. Traveling on a budget is possible; you just have to plan ahead a bit more.

3. I don't know what I need.

The main thing you'll need for traveling within the US are state ID cards (make sure they are Real ID). If you live or are traveling outside the US, get your passports and find out if you need a visa for each country on your list. You will likely need immunizations, depending on your destination. Beyond that, it can be stressful as a parent to anticipate what your child may need, especially when traveling for extended periods of time.

We have included the list we use to pack for Aarav in *Pack Like Mary Poppins*. We have also learned, that even when we forget—or lose—something, most of the time we are able to work around it or find it at a local shop.

4. But my kids' schedule...

Parents often worry that allowing any new behaviors during travel, such as giving kids devices or getting out of a routine, will affect their regular home habits. The good news is that this simply isn't true. Our son went right back to his regular habits within a couple days of returning home. We discuss this topic more in-depth in *Sleeping Nightmares*. Just know that **kids are really flexible** and typically adjust quickly.

5. Travel is too stressful.

Being on vacation doesn't mean everything will be perfect—although it often appears that way in your Instagram feed. **Things will go wrong.** The power might go out, flights could be canceled, your hotel might lose your reservation, your child will have a meltdown in the middle of all the chaos, and the list goes on. As you can see, there are many potential pitfalls. Just because things can go wrong doesn't mean they always *will*. And even if they do, you can still have an amazingly memorable trip.

If you can learn to **roll with it** when things go wrong, you are less likely to have bad experiences when they do. When things get a little tough with our son while we're traveling, we repeat our mantra: "It's just a phase," which we discuss further in *Tales Of Tantrums And Many Cities*.

6. How can I keep my child(ren) occupied?

We suggest using technology. Now, we know the role of technology use for children is a controversial topic. Some parents see no problem with letting their kids play on a phone or a tablet, while others frown upon it.

PLAYING MONKEY PRESCHOOL LUNCHBOX AT A RESTAURANT

"Our personal conviction is that technology can be both useful to you as parents and educational to your children." We used this approach many times on our journey, especially when we needed our toddler to sit still for long periods of time—on a plane, at dinner, or waiting in line.

As we shared in *Our Travel Philosophy: Be F.L.E.X.I.B.L.E.*, we "Embrace Technology" while traveling. On our trips we are a lot more liberal with our use of technology, as long as most of it is educational and informational. Initially, we were afraid that our son would become addicted to the devices while on vacation and would be return home to a world where he simply must have a video on at all times. Thankfully, this hasn't been the case. **Technology was super useful** in our travels, but it hasn't turned our boy into a zombie—not by a long shot. See more on this topic in our section, Using Technology With Kids below.

Using Technology With Kids

Do you remember what it was like in the olden (i.e., pre-iPad) days, when you would go to a nice restaurant with your family? Parents would spend about 60 percent of their time entertaining their children, 20 percent shooting apologetic looks to other diners, 15 percent wondering why they ever thought this was a good idea, and maybe 5 percent enjoying their time there. Well, multiply that by 100 and that is what it can be like to travel with a child. But there is an answer: **Technology.** And we think it's a pretty good one!

Our philosophy around technology

Technology is a big part of everyone's life. There's no avoiding it, and one day, your son or daughter will be using phones and tablets and apps, probably pretty regularly! Since you can't escape technology, we think it's important to be purposeful in how you use it. In fact, by starting your kids on tech early, you can help them acclimate to the

Using Technology With Kids

world they're going to be living in—and potentially even give them a leg up.

Our fears and concerns

It's important to understand that giving your child apps and devices is not without its taboos. We often hear parents declare that they never let their kids use technology. For some, it's a point of pride. That's something you'll probably encounter, too.

We had some of our own concerns. We knew we'd be using technology on our sabbatical, but were worried our son would become addicted. We feared coming home to a world in which he simply must have a video on or some sort of a screen in his hands at all times.

But we were pleasantly surprised when we came back home. He quickly adapted back to a world with less devices and technology. We still allow him to have videos and apps at home (especially when we go out to restaurants), but he often pays little attention to them, and sometimes he actually rejects them altogether.

Our approach and results

We started using technology with our son when he was pretty young; we showed him our iPad to keep him entertained, initially with nursery rhymes, learnings songs, etc. As he got older, we let him play with our phones and learn to manipulate them with a wider variety of apps. We used phones and tablets on our first flight (he was four months old then) and also started using apps in restaurants, just to keep him distracted.

When we left on our nine-month sabbatical, we increased our use of technology significantly. We let our son have apps and videos

Using Technology With Kids

on the plane, in restaurants, and even on certain walking tours. We allowed him to play on apps while we worked out each day. We were cautious though about using technology in the car, as we found that **it can lead to some car sickness.**

Something we discovered early on is that **educational apps and videos tend to really work,** in large part due to the repetition; our son was able to learn letters, words, shapes, numbers, colors, and so much more because of educational technologies that continually repeated concepts in a way that teachers and even parents do not have time to do. At an age where we probably couldn't have told you what a square was, our son was able to recognize a parallelogram, and that is all thanks to the repetitive nature of his favorite apps. Similarly, we have a story from his third birthday, when he walked down the corridors of our cruise ship recognizing the last three digits of the room numbers and screaming out "eight hundred fifty four." That threw us for a loop!

Another thing we noticed is that **apps help children discover new areas for learning** that we didn't even contemplate. Take YouTube for example. Our son would watch a video about numbers, then click on a "related" video that gave him bigger numbers or numbers in a different language—both videos he's never seen before.

Another awesome thing about apps is the sheer number that are out there—and the longevity that each one provides; **kids can use these apps over and over and learn new things each time,** growing in their understanding of concepts and ideas. These apps are scalable as a child grows, and that's pretty cool! We have provided a list of our favorite apps in *Our Favorites* at the end of this book.

Bottom line: Technology enables you to occupy your children without one of the parents having to step out with them. Thus, parents can actually enjoy their time together while still building fantastic experiences with their children.

....

Our final thoughts on fears and excuses.

We strongly believe that your kids follow the example you set, so bring them along on your journey and let them experience the way you live. Give them a taste of adventure and allow them to experience different cultures. It will give them an adventurous spirit, respect for different ways of life, and the wisdom that comes along with all the things they'll experience.

Also remember we tend to make things more difficult than they need to be and use that as an excuse to not do something we really want to do. Or, at the very least, we allow it to postpone our plans. We say, why wait? **Travel now.**

Ready, Set, Prep

Sometimes preparing for a trip can be more stressful than the actual trip. So, in Ready, Set, Prep, **we dive into "Be Prepared" from Be F.L.E.X.I.B.L.E.** and show you how to get the most from your experience by making the preparation go a little more smoothly. We've made plenty of mistakes, and, in doing so, we've learned a few tips and tricks you should implement before leaving that make things a bit easier during your travels.

In *It's All Mental*, you'll learn how to mentally prepare yourself for your upcoming trip and to help prepare your partner as well—and why that's crucial for a successful, happy experience for your whole family. The next step is to prepare your child. Children often thrive in a structured environment, and with travel comes surprises and unexpected circumstances. You'll learn exactly how to prepare your child for these changes, so that he or she is more adaptable once you actually leave.

In *More Money, More Travel, More Problems*, we provide all of our actionable advice on managing your finances while on your trip. Whether you don't know which cards to take on your trip, need to get cash fast while traveling abroad, or want to know how you can keep your money safe while traveling, you'll leave this section feeling fully prepared and knowing exactly what to do with your money while you're away from home.

Finally, in *Pack Like Mary Poppins*, we'll discuss why it's important to pack less than you think you actually need. We know it's tempting to overpack when you're traveling with your children. After all, you want to feel prepared for any situation. By only focusing on the items you actually need, your travel will become easier and, as a result, more enjoyable. To help you along the way, we've also included our comprehensive packing list for kids, which will take out all of the guesswork and leave you feeling ready to embark on your vacation!

So, let's dive in and make the preparation for your trip easy, quick, and fun!

It's All Mental

We are two different types of travelers: One of us (AJ) loves traveling so much that there is no anxiousness—just excitement to encounter new things; the other (Natasha) worries about every aspect of the trip going wrong and wants to be prepared for the worst. Despite those differences, we both fully believe in traveling as a family and having a fantastic time even if there are hiccups here and there.

"Your trip isn't going to be perfect, but imperfectly perfect."

TOGETHER IN PATAGONIA

Preparing yourself

How do you reduce your anxiety about traveling with a child so you can have the best trip possible? First, you need to **mentally prepare yourself** for your upcoming trip. Here are a few of our proven tips to help you do just that:

1. Have realistic expectations.

So many people look at social media and see travel as this beautiful, perfect experience where the family is dressed in cute outfits and carrying a smiling baby—who always looks directly into the camera. The truth is, it's all a dream, and the **reality is a little different.** Most often, you aren't in perfect clothes because your child has spilled something on them. Or, you're in a picture-perfect location, but your child is refusing to take a picture. And if your child is looking at the camera, odds are someone else isn't.

2. Start packing in advance.

Natasha takes the lead in packing for our trips (typically two to three weeks before we travel) because it helps her worry less and she feels she is in control. By thinking of all the things that concern her, she can prepare by packing for things we may need to worry about: what we need if our son gets sick, what we need in our carry-on bags in case luggage gets lost, what we need if we get delayed, etc. We now have a starting-point packing list, and we add to it as needed—including the outfits we'll wear for our not-so-

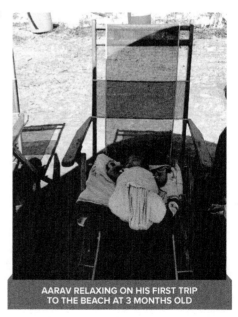

AARAV RELAXING ON HIS FIRST TRIP
TO THE BEACH AT 3 MONTHS OLD

perfect Instagram shots!

3. Take it one step at a time.

The first time you travel with a child is overwhelming because it's so completely different. But every time you travel, **it gets easier.** For our first road trip, we worried about how many diapers to bring, how to buy or store milk for Aarav, and how much to pack. Remember to just take things one step at a time, just as you do in everything you do as a parent. It may feel overwhelming now, but it will get easier.

NATASHA SCARED GOING UP THE CABLE CAR IN THE GREAT WALL

4. Be supportive of each other.

Since AJ doesn't get anxious while flying, he supports Natasha by encouraging her when there is turbulence or by taking care of Aarav on a cable car ride that triggers Natasha's fear of heights. For scenarios like these, AJ has likewise helped mentally prepare Natasha for travel that may be challenging to her. We also both make a point to take turns caring for our son when he gets tired and cranky.

What to Expect on Your First Family Trip

A big part of preparing yourself for the first time you travel with your first child is understanding that you may experience a myriad of feelings while on your trip. Here, we'll try to explain what we felt and give you an idea of the highs and the lows you may feel—and how to navigate them all.

What to Expect on Your First Family Trip

◆ **Expect to feel overwhelmed.** Your first time traveling with your child is bound to feel more overwhelming because you are a new mom or dad. It's okay to be anxious. Just remember to take a breath and try to relax.

◆ **Expect the unexpected.** Diaper blowouts, vomit, and more. It can (and does) happen. When traveling with a very young child, expect to need a little more of their necessities. So, make sure you have enough food, enough diapers, enough of everything they truly need.

◆ **Expect to feel embarrassed.** This is especially true if you are flying, as it might be the first time you feel other people's judgmental glares. If your baby or toddler in the midst of a screaming session, remind yourself of "Focus" from Be F.L.E.X.I.B.L.E. and don't worry about other people. Instead, focus your attention on your child and how you can help him or her return to a calm state.

◆ **Expect to need more time.** Plan to leave earlier and give yourself much more time. Trust us on this one.

◆ **Expect to experience really rough moments.** Your first journey might suck... and that's okay. Remember, the destination will make up for it.

◆ **Expect positive moments, too.** You will remember your first trip/flight forever, so celebrate and commemorate the moments with photos.

Remember that your first experience traveling with your child will be the toughest, so try not to be too hard on yourself and know that it can (and will!) get easier.

Preparing Your Child

Mental preparation also applies to your child.
Although an infant may not understand what changes are occurring when they travel, by the toddler years, you'll want to work to prepare your child for the upcoming trip. Here are five tips to help prepare your child:

1. Talk about the upcoming trip often.

We would talk to our son about how we were going on a plane, what we would be seeing and doing, and what sort of foods we would be trying. **This helped prepare him for the trip** as well as get him excited about the new things he'd experience.

"Talk to your kids about your trip often."

2. Help them visualize the trip.

Young children are often visual creatures. They're learning so much so quickly that helping them to visualize your trip may go a long way in preparing them. So, in addition to talking about the trip, try to "show" your child what the trip will look like. An easy way to do this is to show them videos of your destination(s).

Another great option is to check out or purchase a few travel books specifically tailored to your young child. If your child is three years old or younger, the *Hello, World* book series may be helpful to read to them (and even take along on your trip). Depending on your travel plans, there may even been a book in the series that features your destination (such as *London: A Book of Opposites* or *San Francisco: A Book of Numbers*). Likewise, there are books that focus on specific modes of transportation (such as *My First Airplane Ride*). For children ages 4 and older, we recommend easy reader books such as *This Is How We Do It: One Day in the Lives of Seven Kids from around the World* that focus on different locations or *National Geographic Little Kids First Big Book of the World*.

3. Get them involved.

Little kids love to feel like they're "helping" their parents. So, in an effort to get them excited and prepared for your trip, explain the climate of your destination(s) and let them help pack their own clothes. You could also let them pick out a special new outfit to wear during the trip (perhaps featuring a favorite cartoon character) or pack a few favorite toys for the trip.

4. Explain the difference between home and travel.

Perhaps you are used to having dinner promptly at 6 p.m. at home, followed by bath time, and then bedtime by 8 p.m. On the road, in Spain for example, dinner hours are later, and you may start with snacks at 6 p.m., have dinner at 8 p.m., and do bedtime at 10 p.m., skipping bath time until the morning. **Explain that vacation is different than home** and how things will be different but will return to schedule when you return home.

5. Practice with changes that can be experienced at home.

If you're the type of parent who follows a schedule and limits screen time, and you know there will be less structure while you travel, you need to **start preparing your child for the changes.** If they like structure and don't understand or handle change well, they can be out of sorts. Our sister-in-law never allows screen time—ever—and saved it for a flight. When she gave the device to her kids, they didn't know what to do with it. It didn't have the effect she had hoped for. She learned that she needed to prepare them in advance for screen time (which we highly recommend if your child isn't used to using a device).

Learning how to manage your stress and anxiety and be prepared for a trip is as educational an experience as the trip itself. Although it does take time to mentally prepare yourself and your child for travel, the more you travel, the easier it becomes. Trust us, it's worth it to travel together!

In Cairns, Australia, AJ wanted to take a cable car ride from the rainforest back to the city and forgot to mention it to me (Natasha) until we were on the train going up to the rainforest. I am terrified of heights and immediately panicked. I was able to breathe, recover (after getting angry, of course), remind myself that I had done this before, and mentally prepare for the cable car ride. Thankfully, by the time we got to the cable car, the weather was bad and the ride got canceled. I definitely call that a happy ending! And lesson learned for AJ: Prepare Natasha in advance.

More Money, More Travel, More Problems

When it comes to your money, traveling around the world and outside of your comfort zone can certainly create a sense of worry. Losing your credit cards or being pickpocketed are legitimate fears, especially when you are traveling with your children and need to remain on top of your game as parents. The fear, however, can make you overcompensate when it comes to what you carry.

Visiting as many countries as we have, we've seen it all: remote countries where it was hard to use credit cards, countries with failing economies (which meant cash was hard to come by), and everything in between. Today, we use a system that helps us feel we have control of our money and keeps the worry away.

· ·

Managing cash

> "Use ATMs over money exchanges to get cash."

When it comes to carrying cash, you don't want so little that you are in a bind if you cannot find an ATM, but you don't want so much that if something goes wrong, you lose too much. We found our sweet spot is bringing $500 in cash when we travel to foreign countries and $100 in cash when traveling in the US. If we need more, we can simply use our debit cards at a bank ATM to withdraw more funds.

The great thing about using ATMs in foreign countries is you will receive foreign currency that can be used where you are traveling. When withdrawing from an ATM outside of your country, you will get the best exchange rate even if you have to pay a slight fee for using a different bank. Anyone exchanging cash at the airport or exchange offices will generally get billed higher exchange rates and fees. **They're simply not worth it!** Also, when using an ATM, be sure to only use those associated with an actual bank and not just *any* ATM machine; the fees are typically higher at these random machines and the exchange rates are horrible. If the bank's ATM gives you the option to choose their exchange rate, **decline the option.** Traditionally, those are worse than actual market exchange rates. Trust your bank to provide the best exchange rate.

A word of caution: Countries with high inflation or more rural locations may have less cash available in the ATMs. We learned this lesson in Buenos Aires where we found several ATMs that had run out of cash. We had to visit several machines and finally found an ATM with enough cash. In such countries or locations, be aware and don't let your cash get too low.

Choosing your credit cards

We always carry two different credit card brands and our respective debit cards—so, four cards total. We each have our own debit cards attached to separate accounts, so if one loses their card, the other has an account to dip into. Carrying a different debit and credit card brand each is a good backup plan; otherwise, if we ever needed to cancel a card, it would generally cancel all other cards associated with it.

> *"Your debit card is the most important card you will carry on your trip."*

If you only have one debit account, be sure to lock away or hide your debit card at your nightly accommodations. **Do not walk around with it.** We recommend you only carry a debit card when you need to get more cash. **This is how we split up our cash and cards:**

◆ **AJ's wallet:** Joint Chase credit card, AJ's Bank of America debit card (when we need more cash), and $150 in cash

◆ **Natasha's wallet:** Joint Chase credit card, Natasha's American Airlines credit card, and $100 in cash

◆ **Our passport bag:** All of our passports and important documents, Natasha's Bank of America debit card, and $250 in cash

An important tip: Contact all your credit cards before you leave to let them know you will be traveling, especially if you're traveling outside your home country. This will prevent the companies from stopping a transaction. Most banks and credit cards allow you to schedule travel alerts online.

....

Keeping your money safe

Besides splitting our cards and cash as we explained previously, we take other precautions when carrying cash and cards. **We never carry our passports** once we arrive at our accommodations. Instead, we lock them up or hide them somewhere in our bags in the Airbnb. Also, never carry your original passport with you as you explore a city; instead, have a photocopy to carry in case of an emergency (we typically only carry digital copies of our passport on our phones now).

When out and about with our money, AJ will carry a small wallet **in his front pocket** (never in the back pocket), and Natasha will **use zippered bags** versus open totes to make it more difficult for pickpockets. We also never hang a purse or anything with valuables on the back of our stroller and only keep items we wouldn't mind losing in that bag.

If you do lose your card or other important documents, don't lose your cool. **You have a backup plan.** While it will be an annoying inconvenience, it doesn't need to derail your trip. In the worst-case scenario, most credit cards companies can ship you a new card if you're staying in a location long enough.

If we wrote stories about AJ misplacing his credit card, we would have an entire book (AJ never actually lost his card, though, much to the chagrin of Natasha who wanted him to learn a lesson). In Lima, AJ's wallet had fallen between the cushions of a couch at a restaurant. Of course, we only realized this after we reached another bar. We immediately ran back to the restaurant that was, of course, now closed, but the owners let us in and we found the wallet immediately. Having a backup plan for our money helped us manage the situation and not lose our cool, but finding the wallet was definitely a relief!

Pack Like Mary Poppins

This is one of the most common questions we get. We'll get right to the point. When we say you should pack like Mary Poppins, here's what we mean: **Pack less than you think you need.** Really. You will find that you end up packing things you knew you had to have only

GETTING READY TO BOARD THE TRAIN WITH ALL OUR LUGGAGE IN BERLIN, GERMANY

to realize they aren't needed and are taking up valuable space in your luggage. When a friend of mine first started traveling with her family, they would pack everything they might need. They quickly realized they were overpacking started traveling in a more minimalist style. They pared down so much, they and could go for a week or two with just a small backpack each. Not only did this make their travels easier, but it has also helped them learn to simplify other parts of their lives.

While our family likely can't travel with just a backpack each, we've learned you don't need to pack everything you think you might need. You just need to focus mostly on things you absolutely do need.

If you forget something, it's OK. You can find almost anything you need at a nearby store. **The only things you can't replace are your travel documents.** We suggest that you take a picture of (or scan) your state ID card, passport, birth certificate, and any other important documents, and email them to yourself or upload to a cloud storage provider like Dropbox or iCloud. This way you can access them from anywhere in the world on almost any computer or your phone.

We also protect all our content on our phones including our memories (i.e. our photos and videos) using cloud storage. Since we have Apple iPhones, we use iCloud to sync all our photos and videos automatically as we capture them (it also syncs our contacts, notes, calendars and other useful items). **That way we will preserve our memories no matter what happens** (note: you may have to connect to Wifi to get your latest content to cloud storage; we make sure we do this once a day). We also believe in paying for extra storage if needed and not purging old images and videos or moving it to another storage device that can get lost or corrupted (such as an external hard drive) — it helps keep all our memories together and makes it so much easier to search for several years at a time. Currently, we are paying for the 2 terabyte plan on iCloud ($9.99 a month) and are barely at 300 GB with all of our photos and videos (AJ's phone has almost 60,000 photos and 2,500 videos) — we still have tons of space!

Also, make sure your passports are valid long enough that you will be allowed to enter, and return from, your destination. Most countries have passport expiration requirements before they let you enter, so **check your passport and passport expiration requirements** at your destination at least two months before your trip so you can get a new passport if you need to.

ORGANIZATION MADE EASY USING PACKING CUBES

So, let's dive in and review the five major elements of our Mary Poppins Packing Method!

1. Pack the right gear.

Our biggest tip for packing is to use packing cubes. If you're not familiar with them, you can buy assorted packing cubes in various sizes; these are fully transparent and allow you to section off the items you're packing.

"Use packing cubes to make your life much easier."

For example, you can get a big cube for each parent, a smaller cube for your little one, a cube for swimming gear, and perhaps one for underwear and socks— you get the idea. The best part is it's **always easy to find**

exactly what you want without having to do too much rummaging around or getting your stuff all disheveled.

We'd also recommend having a **plastic bag** in your luggage that you can use for laundry; as you wear clothes and change out of them, just throw them into the laundry bag, ensuring they are kept separate from the clean items.

We strongly recommend getting a travel stroller. Not just any stroller, but a stroller that is lightweight, easy to carry around, and can provide a comfortable place for your child to relax when they are tired or need to go to sleep. A stroller is paramount in helping explore a city, taking your child to a museum, or going on a walking tour. Our favorite travel stroller is the GB Pockit (see more information on this specific stroller plus several other other great travel strollers on our blog ☑). You can take this stroller as a carry-on on the plane! If you have more than one child, see *The More, The Merrier* for recommendations on travel strollers and travel hacks. Before buying a travel stroller, make sure to check any age or weight limits (our recommended travel stroller is for kids over six months of age and can last for years after that!). If your child is below the recommended age or weight limit, we still strongly recommend taking your current stroller/car seat combination since it will make the trip a whole lot easier.

"Should we take a stroller or not?" is the most common question we get from parents. And our answer is a big and unequivocal YES! (We believe in this so much that we've used the word stroller over 70 times in this book 😃).

Something else you should have is a backpack for your child. It doesn't have to be anything special—we just used a normal North Face backpack we found on Amazon—but make sure it's **reasonably spacious.** Try to pack all of your son or daughter's accessories here: toys, books, milk or juice, and so on. One advantage to the backpack is it's easy to hang on your stroller, so it's incredibly portable. And, if your kid is old enough, you can have your child carry his or her own gear! This will give your child a sense of **ownership and control.**

What's more, using the backpack puts some limits on how many toys and books you can bring on your trip—and that definitely can be helpful!

Finally, note that these little backpacks can be your child's airplane carry-on, so it's one less bag you have to check.

Another must-have is a medicine bag. Stock it with Band-Aids, bug spray, sunscreen, antibacterial ointment, Tylenol/Motrin/Benadryl (including kid versions), and some decongestants. A diaper rash cream is also useful to keep here, even if you have no one in diapers. We always have our little medicine bag with us, even when traveling domestically (see our full list at the end of this chapter).

We also recommend taking a small baby monitor, which may come in handy as you settle into an unfamiliar living space; you can use the monitor to make sure your child is falling asleep properly the first night in the Airbnb, for example.

USING OUR BAGGAGE STRAPS

If you have a lot of gear that you will be carrying for a child, we recommend carrying baggage straps (see picture). They can help you move luggage around without needing a cart or additional help. These can be a real back saver.

2. Pack the right clothes.

In addition to packing the right gear, you'll also want to make sure you select the right items to bring along. The hardest part is making sure you bring the right clothes for your child.

"Always get your swim gear no matter the weather."

You don't want to go overboard and bring everything in your child's closet, but do **take clothes that are easy to layer.** Bring at least one pair of pants, even if you're going to a hot area; choosing pants over shorts can provide some good protection against the sun, insects, weeds, and weather. **We also recommend packing at least one jacket**—and if you're going anywhere there's even a chance of colder temperatures, pack both a smaller windbreaker and a heavier winter coat.

Always pack swimsuits no matter the season or the weather. **You never know when your hotel or Airbnb will have an indoor pool.** Our son spent a lot of time swimming all through our travels—a great way to keep him entertained! Similarly, pack any floats your child needs to stay buoyant; our son likes the Stearns puddle jumper.

3. Pack kid-friendly food.

Any time you're packing for kids, you obviously want to bring along some food. We always packed our son's favorite snacks, even things that are easy to find in stores, just so we'd always have them handy. We'd recommend some **emergency chocolate**, too—or whatever food items help your child calm down during a tantrum.

Likewise, **bring some quick meals** you can make on the fly for your child, especially if you show up to a hotel or Airbnb late one night and just need to get some food on the table ASAP. For us, little packets of noodles, requiring only hot water, worked out well.

Our child happens to really like milk. Unfortunately, **milk can be hard to get in certain parts of the world.** Knowing this, we always pack some milk in extra bottles or sippy cups, just to make sure we had some within reach. On occasion this caused a slight delay as we went through airport security, but it was never really a problem. Security just scanned the contents a little more thoroughly before passing us through. While you're traveling, you can usually find milk in coffee shops if you really need to stock up.

Speaking of which, **pack extra sippy cups,** because these can be hard to find overseas, and you never know when your child might throw or lose one!

4. Plan for bathroom needs.
One thing parents may overlook is packing for your child's bathroom needs.

If your child is not potty trained, you clearly need diapers and wipes. Depending on which one of us you ask, you should pack for either a couple or four full days, but rest assured that you can travel anywhere in the world and still find diapers or pull-ups of some kind. **We never had any problem locating diapers or pull-ups for our son.**

If your child is potty trained, you'll want to bring along a portable potty seat. We have written an entire chapter in this book around traveling with a potty-training child. *See Saving Private Poopers* for more information.

5. Consider our carry-on philosophy.
A final point of the packing discussion: How should you pack your airplane carry-on bags?

We feel it's best to **stick with the essentials:** your medicine bag, the portable potty seat (if needed), diapers (if needed), a change of clothes for everyone, and perhaps some minor toiletries—*whatever you'd need to survive* if your luggage (God forbid) gets lost or delayed. Also, bring along anything you need to keep your child, and yourselves, entertained on the plane, like an iPad and a few favorite toys.

In summary
That's our best advice on packing for a trip, and these tips have all worked out well for us. Our biggest tip is to **relax,** and remember, if you need to stop into a store and grab something, that's going to be no big deal.

We made the mistake of not using packing cubes during our big trip across the world. In Victoria Falls (for just two nights) all the clothes we needed were all the way at the bottom of our suitcases, and Natasha had a meltdown pulling them out. If we had packing cubes, we could have easily created a packing cube for a short trip like Victoria Falls!

The 2 Idiots comprehensive packing list for kids

Links to all the products mentioned below plus a printable and downloadable version of this list available exclusively to you at www.the2idiots.com/resources/

☐ Travel stroller (6+ months)

☐ Stroller rain cover (optional depending on weather)

☐ Travel car seat

☐ Travel bassinet/Travel crib (optional)

☐ CARES Airplane Safety Harness (1+ year old and 22-44 pounds)

☐ Baby carrier (for younger kids, 8-32 pounds)

☐ Packing cubes

☐ Baggage Straps (optional)

☐ Youth toy backpack(s) with all their toys and books (Aarav's favorite toys: magnetic drawing board, Mr. Pencil, WOW Water Pad; Aarav's favorite books: The Very Hungry Caterpillar, Goodnight Moon, Brown Bear)

☐ Medicine bag (sun screen, bug spray, antibacterial ointment, Tylenol/Motrin/Benadryl, decongestant, diaper rash cream, Band-Aids, thermometer, antibacterial wipes/hand sanitizer, snot remover)

☐ Travel baby monitor

☐ Devices (iPhone, iPad, Kindle, etc.) —fully charged and charge cords

☐ Earmuffs/Headphones

☐ External battery charger—fully charged

☐ Spare plastic bags (trust us, they will come in handy)

☐ Milk bottles/sippy cups

☐ Food
  ○ Snacks (chips, fruit bars, dry cereal, etc.)
  ○ Emergency chocolate (like M&Ms to give during a tantrum)
  ○ Quick meals like instant noodles (just in case you need it)
  ○ Milk/baby formula/water

☐ Not potty-trained child: 3-4 days' worth of diapers , odor-control diaper bags/plastic bags

☐ Potty-trained child/in potty training: 3-4 days' worth of pull-ups, portable potty seat

☐ Toiletries for child (brush, toothpaste, baby wash, baby lotion)

☐ Swimming clothes and diapers (swimsuit, puddle jumper, swim diapers)

☐ Child clothes
  ○ Must include light jacket
  ○ Might include light pants
  ○ Extra pair of shoes
  ○ Sunglasses

☐ _____
☐ _____
☐ _____

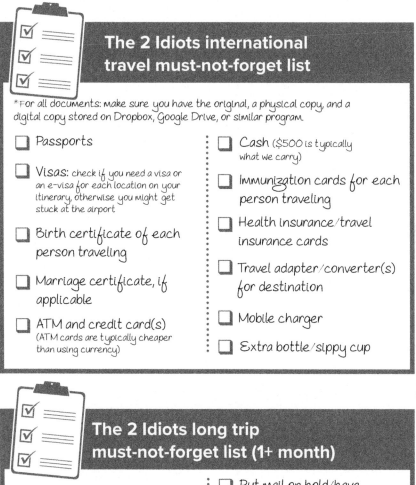

The 2 Idiots international travel must-not-forget list

*For all documents: make sure you have the original, a physical copy, and a digital copy stored on Dropbox, Google Drive, or similar program.

- ☐ Passports

- ☐ Visas: check if you need a visa or an e-visa for each location on your itinerary, otherwise you might get stuck at the airport

- ☐ Birth certificate of each person traveling

- ☐ Marriage certificate, if applicable

- ☐ ATM and credit card(s) (ATM cards are typically cheaper than using currency)

- ☐ Cash ($500 is typically what we carry)

- ☐ Immunization cards for each person traveling

- ☐ Health insurance/travel insurance cards

- ☐ Travel adapter/converter(s) for destination

- ☐ Mobile charger

- ☐ Extra bottle/sippy cup

The 2 Idiots long trip must-not-forget list (1+ month)

- ☐ Spare phone (we bought an iPhone 5 on eBay in case one of our phones broke)

- ☐ Turn off water

- ☐ Turn off gas

- ☐ Extra travel adapters

- ☐ Put mail on hold/have somebody pick up mail-on-hold

- ☐ Put newspapers on hold or have someone collect them for you

- ☐ Put a hold on your car insurance (talk to your insurance agent about this)

We have also made a printable and downloadable version of these lists available exclusively to you at www.the2idiots.com/resources/.

Conquering The Elements

On a boat, in a plane, in a car, or on a train—regardless of how you decide to get there, your next step is to travel to your destination. And while you may have once felt a huge weight lifted off your shoulders when you made your flight or placed your last piece of luggage in your car before a long road trip, that's likely not true now that you're traveling with your child. After all, you've experienced the complaints of your child's boredom, hunger, and discomfort before (and don't even get us started on the toddler tantrums). How do you keep your child happy (and yourself sane) as you embark on your trip?

In Conquering the Elements, **we highlight the importance of "Improvise" from Be F.L.E.X.I.B.L.E.** Remember, traveling often comes with a lot of unknowns, so you'll need to be prepared to go with the flow during your trip. And regardless of what surprises may await you, we're going to show you exactly how to make your travel enjoyable!

In *Buckle Up Fast With Your Boarding Pass,* you'll learn all of our best tips for air travel. We'll discuss how to book the right seats for your family (and how to gain more space for free) with our Plane Seat hacking Strategy. You'll also find tips on when to get to the airport and how to entertain your kids while waiting to board the plane and also during the flight. *Buckle Up Fast with Your Boarding Pass* will leave you fully prepared—and dare we say excited—to take your kids on their next flight.

In *Chuggin' Along In Style,* we discuss everything you need to know about traveling with kids on a train. You'll learn why we prefer train travel over other options and which cars to avoid when you have young children in tow. We'll also review why it's important to get to your platform as quickly as possible and the boarding process we've found most efficient when traveling with our son. When you approach it the right way, train travel is fun and exciting for children—and for adults!

In *Road Trippin',* we discuss how to select the right vehicle for your trip. If you're traveling internationally, it's important to know which cities offer the space for a larger vehicle and which don't. Filled with helpful tips, you'll learn why you should plan trips in the car during your child's naptime or bedtime and how much extra time you should allow for longer drives. Road Trippin' will leave you feeling prepared to hit the road anytime.

In *Wheels On The Bus Go Round And Round,* you'll learn all about bus travel. While we admit that the bus is our least favorite mode of transportation when traveling with children, sometimes it's necessary. So, we'll discuss the best seats you should choose to minimize disrupting other passengers and even how to navigate the potty on a bus with a young child.

Finally, in *Whatever Floats Your Boat,* we'll review the pros and cons of taking your kids on a cruise. We also discuss how to best pack for a cruise, how to set up sleeping arrangements for both larger and smaller rooms, and whether cruise excursions are really worth the cost. Finally, you'll find some helpful tips on planning your time on land so you can make the most of your time off the ship—and also make sure you're back on the boat in plenty of time (we've had a few close calls!).

Buckle Up Fast With Your Boarding Pass

By the time our son was three, we had already traveled enough in planes to make it around the world three times! So, we have some decent experience to share.

GETTING READY TO FLY FROM DUBAI TO BEIJING ON EMIRATES

Air travel can take its toll on all of us. Our recommendations are very practical, but they are not miracles.

· ·

Book the right seats

Many airlines will offer discounted prices if you allow the airline to pick your assigned seat at boarding. While this may save you money, we don't recommend this when traveling with young children. **Make sure you have reserved seating for your family to sit together.** Also, whenever possible we reserve bulkhead seats that give us all a little extra room, and provide our son a little bit of space to play on the floor. On some longer flights, bulkhead seats sometimes give you enough space to set up a small crib for your child to sleep (we talk more about sleeping on a plane and times to book flights in Sleeping Nightmares). Bulkhead seating is great. Whenever you can, book it.

A common question we get is whether to book a separate seat for a child that is under 2 years of age. **Our answer is that it depends—on the duration of your flight, your child (and their size!) and seating availability.** Typically we don't book a separate seat for short flights. However, for longer and/or overnight flights there is immense value in your child having their own space to move around and sleep in. We started booking Aarav his own seat when he was around 18 months of age—he is a relatively tall child and he was most comfortable in his own seat. Finally, prior to booking a separate seat, we always check the seat configurations and availability of seating in advance and tried to employ our Plane Seat Hacking Strategy (described below) and take a shot at getting that extra space for FREE!

AARAV ENTERTAINING OTHER PASSENGERS BEFORE OUR FLIGHT TAKES OFF

One of our most popular tricks for flying with a young child is our Plane Seat Hacking Strategy, designed to give you more space without spending an extra dime! The key for gaining another strategy to gain more space is to find a row (ideally, the bulkhead) that's empty and not book the middle seat. If your child is a lap child, you can do this for a three-seat configuration by booking the window and aisle seats and leaving the middle seat open. Worst-case scenario, somebody else books the middle seat, and they will be happy to switch for a window or an aisle seat.

If your child is not a lap child, then you can try this on a four-seat configuration where you book the two aisles and one of the middle seats, leaving the other middle seat empty. In either situation, odds are decent that you get extra space.

We've found that we're able to use this strategy for about one-third of our trips. So, say you fly three times a year. With the cost of an airline ticket averaging in at $359, if you're able to implement this strategy even just once, you're looking at gaining $1,077 worth of free space over a three-year period! If you have more than one child, see our thoughts on seat selection in the chapter, *The More, The Merrier.*

THE 2 IDIOTS PLANE SEAT HACKING STRATEGY - 1 CHILD

Lap Child   Non Lap Child

2-SEAT CONFIGURATION

3-SEAT CONFIGURATION

4-SEAT CONFIGURATION

Getting to the airport

It's not just the flight that can stress you out when traveling with kids. From the moment you depart for the airport, the stress can begin. Keep calm and carry on by making the first step one of your easiest.

- **Prep your children.** If you have toddlers or older children, explain to your kids what they will see and do at the airport. Tell them about security and lines; make sure they understand what you are about to do.
- **Count your bags.** Know how many pieces of luggage you are traveling with, including your stroller, and keep that number in your head and count your bags every time you are moving from one place to the next to ensure you have all of your gear.
- **Decide whether or not to take your car.** We live pretty close to an airport and find it's much easier to have an Uber or taxi take us directly there, where we can be dropped off right at the door. The flip side is driving to the airport, parking and having to carry all of your bags while managing your child to get to check-in. Economically, if it makes more sense to park, drop off all of your luggage and a parent with the kids at the airport at check-in, and then park the car to make it easier.
- **Get to the airport early.** When traveling with kids, **things take longer.** Be sure you are not rushed and frantic and get to the airport early. We try to be at the gate at least 30 minutes before boarding.

At the airport

Hopefully, you will spend a maximum of two hours in the airport, from checking in, getting through security, and boarding. Whether you have it easy or find yourself delayed, you can make your time at the airport stress-free as well.

AARAV RELAXING IN THE LOUNGE AT BUDAPEST AIRPORT

◆ **Wait in check-in line solo.** Have one parent in line with the luggage at check-in while the other stays with the kids and lets them run around until it's your turn to check in. Your kids are about to sit for a long time on a plane; let them run around and get their energy out before the flight. It's exhausting to chase after your child, but it will make the flight easier.

◆ **Enroll in a global entry-type program.** If you live in a country such as the US with a TSA-precheck program that helps you skip lines at security, enroll! It is a lifesaver for parents at their home airports. You won't have to take off your shoes and unload carry-on bags with your child waiting. Just put everything on the conveyor belt and walk through. Totally worth it! If you fly internationally, having these benefits makes it much easier to get through immigration by skipping the lines.

◆ **Ignore the sighs.** If you do go through security lines, ignore the people around you sighing and rolling their eyes at the family before them. Take your time so you can be sure you don't forget anything and aren't frazzled. This is also a great opportunity to remember to focus on your child and family. **You'll never see those** people again anyway.

◆ **Fill up water bottles.** Carry a few empty bottles and fill them with water before your flight. The airport knows they have a captive audience and charges three to four times more for bottled water, so having your own empty bottles you can fill will save you money.

◆ **Get food.** Yes, flights may offer food, but when you are traveling with a child always stop and get food. You never know how long the flight will sit on the runway or be delayed. Get food; hungry kids = cranky kids.

◆ **Take advantage of lounges.** If you have the right credit card, you may have access to airport lounges. You will find food and drinks that you can enjoy, and in most, kids are welcome. We love the Chase Sapphire credit card, which provides lounge access all around the world for card members in the US.

◆ **Exhaust the kids.** Use the time at the airport to wipe out your children before the flight, which will help them sleep or stay in one place once they are on the plane.

"Exhaust your kids before you get on the plane."

AARAV ENJOYING THE PLANES COMING IN AND OUT AT CHARLOTTE AIRPORT

Here are five ideas of things to do at the airport to exhaust your kids:

1. Have them walk in the airport vs. sitting in the stroller.
2. Find the airport play area (most airports have one) and let your children play.
3. Watch planes take off and land.
4. Find gate numbers/letters and play alphabet/counting games.
5. Escalators or elevators up and down make fun rides for kids (be careful with escalators!).

The more you can exhaust your kids, the easier the flight will be!

Before you board and pre-flight

Before the flight, those last few minutes of boarding, strapping in, and taking off can also be harried and stressful. To make it easier:

GETTING READY TO FLY TO PATAGONIA ON AEROLINAS ARGENTINAS

- ◆ **Use the family bathroom.** Before you board, use the family bathroom and change diapers or go to the bathroom one more time before you are restricted on the plane.
- ◆ **Get on the flight early.** Most airlines offer priority boarding to families with young children. Take advantage of this and board early. You also want to be sure there is enough space for all of your carry-ons, including that travel stroller that you can take on to the airplane! We put our folding travel stroller into a shoe bag just to avoid any issues with gate-checking it. (While most airlines now are familiar with carry-on strollers, there are still airlines such as Argentina's Aerolineas Argentinas where we ran into issues with carrying it on.)
- ◆ **Buckle in last.** Don't force your child to sit; instead buckle him or her in only once you absolutely must. We typically wait for the plane to start moving and then buckle him in.

What to carry on?

The first thing we recommend is **getting an FAA-approved harness.** We highly recommend the CARES Airplane Safety Harness (be careful when you search for this item on Amazon; there are a lot of knockoffs around. This harness is the one that says "Kids Fly Safe" on top of it's packaging). This device is designed to make it easy for your child to sit in their own seat comfortably. It also allows them to sleep on the plane, which is essential—especially on an overnight flight that coincides with your little one's bedtime. Additionally, it gives your small child extra protection if you

AARAV IN A CARES AIRPLANE SAFETY HARNESS

encounter turbulence. Because this harness is only for children over a year old, we carried our son on our laps when he was an infant and used the lap belt provided by the airline.

When flying, we always take one small backpack for our son. In his bag he carries his toys and books and a few snacks (see what Aarav likes on our packing list in *Pack Like Mary Poppins*). **Find things that keep your child entertained**, ideally with minimal noise and not too many moving and small parts. Don't forget to load some educational apps onto your devices. If your child uses headphones, don't forget to bring those so he/she can use it on the flight (Aarav didn't like headphones when he was younger and watched the videos on low volume). We subscribe to YouTube Premium, which has a lot of great, kid-friendly channels and videos that can be downloaded for offline viewing. Downloading content from Netflix also works, though we honestly found more good stuff on YouTube. On the day of the flight, we limit the amount of time Aarav has on the devices until we get on the plane and actually need the distraction. And if you are still looking for other ideas to keep your kids entertained, check out 12 Tips To Entertain Your Child On The Plane.

As we shared in the previous chapter, if your child is potty trained, we recommend bringing along a portable potty, which can make the entire process a bit easier. And if you're in a situation where your child needs to go, and you feel like you can't get up (if the seatbelt sign is on, for example) ring for a flight attendant. They were always understanding with our son and happy to help.

· ·

Other tips

"Ensure you have enough milk before boarding the plane."

One thing we learned the hard way is... *a lot of international flights don't have milk.* If your child needs milk for the flight, be sure to bring extra or buy some in the airport just before you board. If you can't find any at a convenience store, try a coffee shop. And naturally, you'll want to take plenty of snacks, especially on long flights—but that's something most parents won't need to be told!

If your child's ears hurt due to **changes in air pressure**, try giving him/her a bottle or pacifier to suck on to help release the pressure. If your child doesn't like a bottle or pacifier, give him something to chew and swallow like a small soft candy. Make sure you have these things handy especially during takeoff and landing and give them to your child frequently, so the pressure doesn't build up.

We were lucky to travel business class on one of our flights and Aarav started using the leg rest as a slide. He spent hours playing on it – seriously, kids will make a toy out of anything! On a future flight, we were sitting in economy as we typically do, and he searched everywhere for a leg rest so he could make another slide 😄. Seems like he gets used to fancy things—just like his mom!

12 Tips to Entertain Your Child On The Plane

Just imagining keeping a child still for three straight hours or more is enough to scare parents away from traveling with kids, but with more than 70 flights under our belts, we have found ways to keep our son entertained on flights.

Read books.
We always travel with at least four of our child's favorite books in our carry-on. See our packing list in Pack Like Mary Poppins above for some ideas.

Do an activity.
We try to give our son sitting activities as much as we can, like coloring and activity books and a drawing board.

Play magnetic travel games.
Typically, games intended for the car or plane are small and often made with magnetic pieces to make it easier to play without pieces flying about. Here are a couple of ideas: HABA Town Maze Magnetic Game or the HABA Number Maze Magnetic Game which is a STEM version.

Bring surprise toys.
A trick a friend likes to do is to wrap small toys in foil and to bring one for each hour they are on a plane. This allows their child to open something new every hour and leads to fun distractions. You can't bring gift-wrapped items through airport security, so foil makes it easy to open for both security and your child.

Pull out the with Play-Doh.
There's a reason Play-Doh has been so popular with children for almost 70 years. Kids love to use their imaginations and create their own mini sculptures in vibrant, fun colors.

12 Tips to Entertain Your Child On The Plane

Play with slime.

This non-sticky Play-Doh alternative is all the rage with kids right now. So, why not utilize it when you need to distract your child during a flight? Keep a brand-new pack of slime as a surprise and pull it out for your child when he or she starts to become bored to buy yourself some extra time until you land.

Two cups of ice and a plastic spoon.

Yes, this sounds silly, but our son has a fascination with ice and plastic cups and spoons. He loves to move the ice cubes back and forth between cups. Yes, it's a little messy, but it's just water and easily cleaned up.

Tune into the in-flight entertainment.

Most international flights have in-flight entertainment at each seat that includes children's programming and games. Our son loved to press the buttons on the screen.

Look out the plane window and count clouds.

While AJ jokes that there are millions of clouds, that is the point. You can spend so much time counting clouds and practicing numbers as well as searching for clouds that look like unique animal shapes.

12 Tips to Entertain Your Child On The Plane

Walk around.

If the seat belt sign is off, take advantage of it, and take mini walks down the aisles of the plane, especially back to the cabin crew area where they love kids and may offer a snack. And do it as soon as that seat belt sign turns off prior to the drink and meal service.

Turn to electronic devices.

We do not recommend just handing your kids an electronic device for the duration of the flight. Instead, we use these for emergency breakdowns or when we need a break. See Don't Leave Home Without These Apps in Our Favorites.

Have a secret stash of candy.

Our go-to when our son couldn't take one more minute on a plane was simply ten M&Ms. Yes, we were bribing him, but it immediately calmed him down and saved us on many occasions.

Chuggin' Along In Style

> Our #1 Choice

I f we had to pick our favorite way to get around, we'd pick train travel in a heartbeat. We find it to be far more comfortable than plane, bus, or car travel. There's more space to get up and walk around and no turbulence or air pressure changes. Most trains get you where you need to go pretty fast, yet there's ample opportunity to look out your window and take in the scenery.

AARAV ENJOYING HIMSELF ON THE TRAIN JOURNEY FROM ROME TO FLORENCE, ITALY

You don't have to show up hours in advance; you don't have to go through rigorous security procedures. Sometimes you can get a whole cabin just for you and your family. Even if you don't get a cabin, you can usually get seats that face one another, often clustered around a table.

To get the most out of your long-distance train travel—especially when you have a toddler in tow—we have a few simple tips.

Preparation

Make sure you actually **purchase a seat for your child.** Some trains will offer free tickets for your child, but not an actual seat. Trust us, you'll want the seat, especially for long trips.
Some trains have entire cars that are designated as quiet cars. You probably want to **avoid these** as kids (and some adults) are not known for being reliably quiet.

"Purchase your child their own seat on the train."

A lot of trains offer first- and economy-class seating, and while the price for first-class is more expensive (you may end up paying 30 percent more for your **first-class upgrade**) we think it's totally worth it.

At the train station

The good thing about train stations is there is a lot to do. Sometimes there are open areas with pigeons you can feed, escalators to ride, and trains coming in and out to watch. It's high-energy and interesting to children.

♦ **Arrive early.** Get to the train station **one hour to a minimum of 30 minutes** before your train departure time to ensure you get through the station and find your platform with enough time to spare. They may have security checks, such as one we encountered in Seville that added another 10 minutes to our time.

♦ **Grab food.** If there is food at the station, stock up on snacks and milk for your ride. However, remember that long train journeys offer food carts or snack bars so you should be okay regardless.

◆ **Get to the platform ASAP.** While you can enjoy the station and let your child exert a lot of energy, as soon as your platform is announced, get to it. Sometimes the train platform won't be announced until just before the train departure time, so one parent needs to be keeping an eye on the platform boards. When you make your way to the platform, have one parent manage your children while the other manages the luggage. **(Don't forget to count every piece so you keep track and make sure you have everything!)**

WAITING AT THE PLATFORM FOR THE TRAIN IN ZURICH, SWITZERLAND

Once you are at your platform, find the location your train car will be at, which is generally marked on the platform, or ask an employee to direct you if it's confusing. If you can get to your specific train car 10 minutes in advance you generally will be one of the first people to board the train which makes it a whole lot easier.

• •

Boarding the train

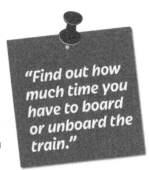

"Find out how much time you have to board or unboard the train."

If you are at a platform at the main train station from which a train originates, it's much easier than when you have to catch a train in the middle of the route. If you are at the first station, the train is already on the platform, you just board and you leave. Voila!

But, what if you are at that middle station? Some trains give you a minute or two to board (see our story below). That's it. Just a minute or two—with children! Although it may feel daunting to only have a couple of minutes to board, if you are prepared, it really can be quite easy.

Here are four tips to help you make this a breeze:

◆ **What if you are standing in the wrong spot?** Imagine the train arrives and for some reason, you are standing in the wrong spot with your correct train car five or six cars away. This has happened to us a few times, and it can be nerve racking.

Here is our plan to handle this situation: We try to determine if we should move to the correct car while on the platform, or board the train and then move to the correct car from the interior. While the trains interconnect, carrying bags through the train is much more difficult than doing so on the platform. If we have more than three minutes to board the train, we will move along the platform to our car or to the car closest that we can get to with two minutes to go, always keeping an eye on the time. If we have less than two minutes to board, we will board the nearest car we are at and then move between cars.

◆ **Board your kids first.** When we are waiting on the platform, we will put Aarav into his stroller so when the train arrives, we can quickly get him onto the train. Board your children first and have one parent stand on the train at the door to keep it open as the other parent loads luggage onto the train.

◆ **Never leave children alone.** Never, ever leave your children alone on or off the train. One parent should always stay with the children. If, for some reason, one parent misses the train, you can always catch up on the next train, but, in the meantime, your children are with a parent.

◆ **Do the reverse when you arrive at your destination.** When it's time to get off your train, once again you may have only mere minutes. Start bringing your bags to the door four to five minutes before the stop so you are in front of the door and ready to disembark as soon as you stop. Do everything as you would for boarding but in reverse: Get your children off first with a parent, then have one parent get all the luggage off as the other helps and stays with the children.

Other train passengers are also typically very helpful in these situations, especially when seeing a family attempting to embark or disembark. For first-time train families, we know it can seem overwhelming, but the more you ride, the easier it becomes.

On the train

Once you get on the train (phew!), it gets a whole lot easier and a whole lot more fun!

You can **get up and walk around the train with your child**—something your child will really love! It eats up some time and keeps everyone from going stir-crazy. We also enjoy just looking out the window together as the train passes through different types of terrain. And don't forget that many trains have lunch cars—not just a good place to mingle and stretch your legs but perhaps also to have a quick drink or two! Also, if you need to, make sure you follow some of the same types of toys and tips we recommend for plane travel above.

As part of our long adventure, we took a train from Tokyo to Kyoto. The Japanese are super punctual, and we only had two mins (gulp) to board the train. Needless to say, with our large collection of luggage and restless child two minutes was not going to be enough. It turned out we were wrong, and two minutes is an eternity when you are boarding a train. We were able to make it onto the train with plenty of time to spare!

Road Trippin'

Over nearly nine months of international travel with our two-year-old, we spent plenty of time in the car. We rented vehicles in several countries and explored our surroundings via automobile, always with our little man along for the ride. We also had several tour guides who carted us around in their vehicles, so our experience in this regard was quite varied.

AARAV IN THE IMMI GO CAR SEAT WITH HIS MOM AND COUSIN IN AUSTIN, TEXAS

Here are a few ways to keep everyone as safe—and as sane—as possible.

It's important to **select the right vehicle.** Generally speaking, we'd encourage you to consider an SUV—though there are plenty of exceptions. In Europe, for example, we found that the streets were so narrow that driving and parking an SUV could be truly frustrating. In countries where SUVs make sense and we'd include the US, China, India, and many Central and South American nations here—try to get one. For one thing, these vehicles are on the heftier side—so if an accident did happen, you'd have a certain level of built-in safety. SUVs are also a little more spacious, meaning you can get car seats, luggage, and people in and out with greater ease.

At many rental places around the world, we found that the base-level car was manual transmission. Always double-check this! Don't just assume that the car you're getting has an automatic transmission.

"Check your rental for manual vs. automatic transmission."

Car seats are not required in all countries, but we recommend carrying one anyway. You won't regret this extra level of protection for your child. Similar to the travel stroller, we recommend buying the IMMI GO car seat (get more information on this travel car seat and other recommend car seats on our blog ⧉) that is easy to carry around and is also foldable! If there are age and weight restrictions, bring their regular car seats - car seats always get free check-in at most airports and can be strapped to luggage to be carried around.

Save some money by only renting cars for longer distances and using other methods of travel when exploring cities.

As you drive long distances with a toddler, you'll want toys your child can hold and play with on their own. Bring a bag for your toddler loaded with their favorite books and toys plus a few downloaded shows and educational apps. (For more ways to keep kids entertained during long car rides, see Top Road Trip Activities For Kids on the following page.) Also, don't forget to watch your child for symptoms of carsickness, especially on curvy or winding roads.

Top Road Trip Activities For Kids

Here are some of our parent-tested and kid-approved activities guaranteed to entertain your child while you're driving.

◆ **Create your own MusicFest.** This may sound like a no-brainer, but playing music in the car can be a lifesaver. Aarav loved listening to music on our trips (especially Bollywood music!)— and it kept him preoccupied for hours. Find a style of music or a specific artist your child loves to listen to, and just let it play. Plus, this comes with a major bonus: You can take some much-needed downtime since your child will be distracted and happy.

◆ **Play an audiobook.** Plan ahead and download a few kid-friendly audiobooks, such as the Ramona Quinby collection or the Magic Treehouse collection. If you decide this is a great option for you, have your child start listening to some of them now, so he or she is familiar with them. The last thing you want is to have your child screaming because they don't understand what's playing. **Be Prepared!**

◆ **Plan to stop.** When traveling with your child, it's almost a guarantee that your trip will take longer than if you were traveling alone or with another adult. Sometimes a child just needs a break from riding for a little while. If you find that's the case, search for a fast food restaurant with an indoor play ground, such as McDonald's or Chick-Fil-A. Trust us: Letting your child run around and expel some energy for 30 minutes is a much more attractive option than listening to them scream for that same amount of time.

◆ **Get interactive.** Look, we understand that it's easier (and maybe even more appealing) to just set up the iPad and let your child veg out while you're driving. But, believe it or not,

Top Road Trip Activities For Kids

your child will get tired of starting at that screen at some point. And even if he or she doesn't, traveling as a family is all about spending valuable time together and making memories. So, look at your road trip as an opportunity to interact with your kids in fun ways. We personally like to play games as a family. Here are a few to choose from depending on your child's age:

- **Simon Says.** In this game, player one becomes "Simon" and issues instructions to other players. The players must follow the instruction, but only when "Simon" states "Simon says" before stating the instructions. Players are eliminated if they follow an instruction without hearing "Simon says." The last player standing is the winner.

- **Hangman.** Using a pen and some paper, player one thinks of a word, which is represented by a row of dashes (one dash for each letter). Player two has to guess the word one letter at a time. For each wrong guess, a body part is drawn of a hanged man. If player two correctly identifies all letters or the word before the hanged man is fully drawn, they win. If not, player one wins.

- **20 Questions.** Player one picks a person, place, or thing and has player two guess what it is by asking 20 questions. If player two figures out what the person, place or thing is within 20 questions or less, he wins. If not, player one wins.

- **I Spy.** Player one takes on the role of the "spy" and states, "I spy with my little eye, something...." Each time, the spy states a different quality or characteristic describing the item in question. Player two has to guess the item the spy saw. The game continues until player two guesses the item.

Top Road Trip Activities For Kids

- **Memorizing License Plates.** Players can play together or competitively to see license plates from as many different states (or countries) as possible.

Whether you're going to be driving a relatively short distance or you're planning a cross-country trek, try some of our top road trip activities for a peaceful and enjoyable car ride.

Whenever possible, try to leave for car trips around nap or bedtime. If you can't, do what you can to tire your child before the trip. Getting little ones to sleep during the car ride makes things easier on everyone, and when you get to your destination, your child is happy and ready for adventure.

Snacks are, as ever, essential, and **we recommend packing dry stuff,** like chips, that your kids can eat by themselves with minimal stickiness.

For every three hours of driving, plan for an extra 30 minutes—to stop for food, gas, bathroom breaks, or to give everyone a few minutes out of the vehicle.

"Leaving around nap-time makes shorter trips a breeze."

As we reviewed in Top Road Trip Activities For **Kids,** a quick break can do wonders. If your child is potty training, stop more frequently or consider having them wear a pull-up for the trip.

We were driving through Southern Spain in a rental car that we were told was diesel. We stopped at a petrol station and forced a diesel nozzle into the gasoline tank (oops!). Upon starting the car, the dashboard lit up with a ton of alerts, and the car wouldn't accelerate properly. We stopped at the next station and topped it off with gasoline. Luckily, we had only filled it with a few liters of diesel. Lesson learned: Check the car yourself to see if it is diesel or petrol, and don't force a diesel nozzle into a gasoline tank.

Wheels On The Bus Go Round And Round

Bus travel has its perks, including affordability, and its drawbacks—especially when you're traveling with a toddler. Two of the drawbacks: Most of the time you'll be sharing the bus with quite a few strangers, and **buses are usually not equipped with all the child-wrangling supplies you're accustomed to.** For these reasons and many others (such as the nauseating nature of bus travel down bumpy roads), buses represent our least favorite way to travel.

A short bus ride that takes you just a few city blocks is no big deal and usually easily navigable but for longer distances, we have a few tips and suggestions.

"Use bus travel only if you don't have any other option."

Just like trains and planes, we recommend trying to book your toddler their own seat—their own space where they can stand, lay out their toys, and just be comfortable.

We discovered that some bus lines will actually require kids under a certain age to be in a car seat. They go by age, not weight—an important distinction. They literally won't let you on if you don't have a car seat. But here's the rub, the buses don't always have a way for you to attach foldable car seats, which means you need a big, bulky car seat. Try to fit that in your carry on! Before you buy bus tickets, **check for car seat requirements.**

Unless sitting in the front helps you keep from feeling nauseated, we'd generally recommend **sitting in the back of the bus** where your child might be a little less disruptive to other passengers. Even if you don't typically experience car sickness, we suggest packing some Dramamine tablets in your bag.

Of course, **buses aren't likely to have snacks,** and they certainly won't have milk, so pack whatever food and drinks you need. Obviously, eating a meal before you board is ideal.

We were on a one of our rare bus rides from Santiago to Valparaiso, Chile- about a 90 minute drive. Aarav was being particularly difficult on the bus and we had resorted to giving him the iPad. The iPad somehow lost all the downloaded videos and we were both panicked with a screaming child and twenty-five bus passengers glaring at us. I'm sure they weren't actually glaring, but it sure felt like it at the time. We both stayed calm. AJ focused on Aarav, and Natasha was able to connect the iPad to the internet via her iPhone hotspot and got the videos to reappear.

Whatever Floats Your Boat

Imagine this scenario. You have two weeks of vacation. It's the only vacation time you have all year and you want to make it count. You know you want to go to Europe, and you are presented with the option to take a cruise—10–12 nights, departing from Barcelona and hitting ports all over the Mediterranean. You will get to see some sights in France, Italy, Greece, and beyond. Your other option is to fly directly into a city—let's say, Athens—and see Santorini and Mykonos, spending a few nights in each place.

AARAV ENJOYING A BEAUTIFUL SUNSET ON A CRUISE SHIP

It's a tough choice, right? If you take the cruise, you see several places but have less time to explore each. You can't be as flexible since you're bound by the schedule of the cruise ship. In the second option, you see fewer places, but can spend more time in each and have more room to be spontaneous.

It just so happens that we really like cruises. We have been on several cruises—AJ's been on eight, Natasha on seven. We actually like cruises even more now that we have a son. Quick word of advice: Check your cruise line's policy on kids as some cruises have age restrictions.

....

Making the cruising decision

Let's start with six pros to cruising.

1. It's easy and relaxing. Natasha, who handled the packing and day-to-day organization on our trip, found cruises especially relaxing. Most cruise ships have sea days, which offer a good balance: you'll get to see a lot of sights on the cruise but also have some downtime.

"Cruising is an easy and fun way to travel with kids."

ENJOYING TIME WITH AARAV IN THE POOL OF OUR MEDITERRANEAN CRUISE SHIP

2. You avoid visas and day passes. Cruises often mean you don't have to get visas for every place you want to visit, and your day passes are usually handled by the cruise line.

3. You get to see a lot. One of the big advantages to taking a cruise is that it helps you get a better sense for the places you'd like to spend more time. For instance, we had brief visits in Vietnam and Cambodia and very much want to return there. Meanwhile, there are some Scandinavian cities we experienced and enjoyed but don't feel any special need to revisit. Cruising also allowed us to see some magical places we never would have seen otherwise.

4. It's a resort-style experience. Of course, cruise ships have many built-in amenities, including food, bar service, fitness centers, casinos, spas, pools, nightly entertainment ... the list goes on. You can really be pampered on a cruise line—and again, it's all very conveniently available to you.

5. It's great for kids. Cruises are great for kids because of the variety of activities available to them. In addition to the pool areas, many cruises

AARAV PLAYING IN THE DAY CARE ON THE CRUISE SHIP

have mini-golf courses, basketball courts, ping-pong tables, and so much more. Also, almost all cruise lines have daycare centers that provide free childcare, which is great because it gives your kids space to have some fun, and if your child is old enough, you can leave them and enjoy some adult-only time! Cruises will also give you access to 24/7 kids' menus—so you can get your little traveler a slice of pizza, a sandwich, or a cookie anytime you need to.

6. There's an abundance of food. Cruises are known for their exorbitant amounts of food. Buffets are available all day and night. We never had an issue finding something for our son to eat. Most cruise lines also offer fine dining options. Several nights we fed our son at the buffet, dressed him for bed, put him in his stroller, and enjoyed an excellent meal while he slept peacefully next to us.

With all of that said, there are also some cons to taking a cruise.

1. You don't get to spend much time in any one place. Cruises allow you to stop in different cities, but you typically don't have more than a day there, and sometimes you only have a few hours. If there are several things you want to see and do, it can be frustrating.

2. Cruises can be expensive. For those on a tight budget, cruises may not be for you. You may get an initial price that seems reasonable, but when you add in other costs—excursions, drink packages, photo packages, tips, you name it—it can really add up. You can end up spending a few hundred dollars a day, which can be several times more than what you'd pay just getting an Airbnb somewhere and seeing sights on your own.

3. The food. The food you'll get on your cruise is usually fine, but it's not as authentic as what you'd get if you stopped in an actual, local city. Experiencing local food is one of our favorite parts of traveling, so this is definitely a drawback for our family.

4. You can get seasick. We're pretty lucky in this regard, but extreme seasickness is a deal-breaker for others. If you've never been on a cruise and aren't sure whether you'll experience seasickness, we highly recommend taking some medicine with you, just in case. Starting with a shorter cruise on a larger ship is also recommended. Claustrophobia can sometimes be an issue; though these ships tend to be big, the hallways can be cramped and the cabins aren't that big.

Packing for a cruise

We suggest you start first by looking at our chapter *Pack Like Mary Poppins*. Here are some additional packing tips that are specific to cruising:

◆ **Get a travel stroller.** Cruise ships are very large, and getting from point A to point B can be exhausting; you will want a stroller.

◆ **Take a light jacket.** Even if you travel during the summer to the Caribbean, the interior of a cruise ship is often kept chilled, so you'll want a light jacket or a baby blanket to ward off the chill.

◆ **Don't forget swimming items.** Kids love water (except at bath time), and cruise ships offer hot tubs and swimming pools in which kids will want to play. Even if you think it's not warm enough, bring a swimsuit, just in case.

◆ **Take your baby gear.** Cruises don't have restrictions on how much baggage you bring aboard, so bring as much as you want (although space in your cabin could be limited for storage). Bring wipes, diapers, and formula. Overpack essential items as you never know if a shop will have what you need, and you won't want to spend your excursion/onshore days shopping for supplies. Use the no-baggage-limit rule to your advantage.

◆ **Bring the Pack 'n Play.** While most cruise cabins are very small (some too small for a Pack 'n Play), we loved having this during bedtime.

Cruises are fun for all ages and a great way to visit multiple locations without having to book accommodations and get travel visas for each place. The food is never-ending, and there are so many activities no one in your crew will be bored. **Cruising may be the best vacation your family has ever been on.**

We tend to get carried away enjoying cruise destinations. We have almost missed our cruise ship twice (almost being the keyword). In Bangkok, our Uber missed an exit because AJ was too busy reading and NOT paying attention. This was a long highway no U-turns and we had to take a MUCH longer route which made us 45 minutes late. Once we got to the port, we got lost and couldn't find our ship (the port was huge with multiple terminals, some miles apart). We couldn't ask anybody for directions or help because of the language barrier! We were so panicked—what do we do regarding our travel documents (we did have digital copies on our phone as a backup), what about kids stuff, do we get a hotel, how were we going to reconnect with the ship—all kinds of questions going through our mind!

We were so lucky because it just so happened that a couple of the ship's excursions were also late due to the traffic, and because they were associated with the ship, they had to wait for them to return. Since we had an active data plan (T-mobile for the win!), the cruise ship called us during our panic and told us there was nothing to worry about; they would wait for us. It didn't make it better, because we were still lost and frustrated, but at least we didn't miss the boat. We definitely learned a few valuable lessons: pin the ship's location in Google Maps and ensure we get back to the ship at least 45 minutes early.

Surviving the Trip

There are so many things to consider when traveling: accommodations, tickets, tours, strangers, passports, tantrums, accidents, illness—the list goes on and on. While it may seem a bit daunting, we're here to help calm your fears and provide all the know-how you need to successfully navigate your trip as a family.

While Surviving The Trip pulls from almost every principle in our Be F.L.E.X.I.B.L.E. philosophy, **we feel that "Learn" is the foundational principle for this section.** In the coming chapters, we share our mistakes and triumphs so that you can learn how to make your own travels go more smoothly. This section is all about providing our most helpful tips and tricks so you're prepared to overcome any possible frustrating experience and create wonderful memories that will last for years to come.

3. Finally, on the extremely rare occasion that **we couldn't find an Airbnb** in a particular area, that we want to stay in.

Before we get into staying in Airbnbs, here are some tips for staying in a hotel that we've learned along the way, room selection being the most important.

Staying in a hotel

Choosing the right room

The first thing you need to do when selecting a hotel is **figure out your sleeping arrangements and book accordingly.** There are three ways to book rooms in a hotel with kids: you can have just one room, you can have two rooms to accommodate more kids (expensive), or you can have a suite,

AMAZING SUNSET VIEW FROM AJMAN SARAY HOTEL

which is one bedroom with a living area (could be expensive, as well).

If you co-sleep, selecting a room is easier; just select a single room with a king bed, if traveling with one child, or double beds if traveling with multiple children. However, if you aren't cosleeping, like us, we prefer—and strongly recommend—suites, because they provide a separate bedroom and living room. Our son goes to sleep much earlier than we do, so having to share one room can be very difficult. We like suites because we put our crib into the bedroom and put him to sleep, then sit in the living room until we are ready for bed. If you have more than one kid, they can often accommodate a rollaway bed, or you might have to book multiple rooms at that point.

We have described how to handle sleep time in *Sleeping Nightmares*.

Managing Food

Every stay at a hotel means every meal is outside of your accommodations; you must leave the room to get breakfast, lunch, and dinner, as opposed to an Airbnb, where you have a kitchen and the ability to cook. Hotels also offer room service—a special treat! We love to take advantage of room service for breakfast. Sometimes Aarav wakes up too early and restaurants aren't open or we don't want to have to get dressed to go to breakfast (by that time, he's pretty hungry!). Having room service allows us to ease into our morning.

"Don't forget to ask for a microwave in your hotel room."

When we stay at a hotel, we look for those that offer included breakfasts, especially buffets, as well as kids eat free rates to help offset our food budget, since dining out can cost more than when we cook. To help eliminate eating out for breakfast, again, due to our early mornings, **we try to find rooms with microwaves and mini fridges,** then shop at the local store for things we can keep in the room and make for breakfast or kids' meals, like waffles or instant noodles. Sometimes hotels don't offer microwaves in each room, but if we call and ask for one, they usually can accommodate us. Also, make sure to **ask the hotel staff to empty the mini bar** so it can be used as a fridge for milk and other foods.

Entertaining Your Kids

Obviously, when staying at a hotel, you have more offerings than in an Airbnb, such as swimming pools and beach cabanas. Such as was the case with the Atlantis Resort where there are tons of kids' activities like water parks, animal programs, aquariums, kids' clubs, arts and crafts, and play areas. If you're staying at a hotel, definitely take advantage of everything you get and use the amenities during your stay!

If you are staying at a hotel simply for convenience, such as near an airport, go bare bones and use the hotel only for sleeping. You could be in a city enjoying more sites versus swimming in the hotel pool, so no need to spend extra money on amenities you won't be using.

Airbnb

On our big trip across the world, we went to almost a 100 different destinations, and **we used Airbnb for most of them.** Overall, it was an incredibly positive experience. And now we know how to use Airbnb effectively.

Choose the right Airbnb

We generally didn't book any Airbnb without making sure it had **plenty of reviews** (we look for 5 reviews at a minimum) and that those reviews were **fairly positive** (we of course prefer 5 star ratings overall but are okay with 4.5 stars if it seems like a one-off situation in the reviews). For those properties that didn't have many reviews, we would only pick one if it was being managed by a Superhost. (Per Airbnb: Superhosts are experienced hosts who provide a shining example for other hosts, and extraordinary experiences for their guests.) While you may miss out on newly listed properties with fantastic views, **when traveling with kids, it's best to go with the safer bet.**

INCREDIBLE VIEW FROM OUR AIRBNB IN VANCOUVER, CANADA

Generally speaking, rentals that are in the heart of the city will be pricier than those on the outskirts or in the suburbs. However, when you stay in the heart of the city, you can save on transportation costs *and* have more time available to see the sights—so for us, it's totally worth it. Look for lodging that puts you closest to the places you want to explore.

The great thing about Airbnb is that you generally start with a suite-type apartment and can go up to several bedrooms in the same place **so there is plenty of room for your entire family.** Since we don't co-sleep with our child, we preferred to book two-bedroom apartments since that provides the most flexibility and Aarav can have his own separate room. We spend more time discussing sleeping arrangements in *Sleeping Nightmares.*

Save money on great locations

It's a little risky, but if you can wait until the eleventh hour to book, you can save some serious money. Many people cancel their Airbnb rentals at the last minute making great units suddenly available. **We often booked just a day or two in advance and got 10 to 15 percent off the normal rates.** Before doing this, verify there are enough Airbnb's still available two to three days prior to your trip.

Your host

In Argentina, we asked our host how the locals drink their tea and were able to soak up some local customs and cultures through that single question.

"Take advantage of your host and their local knowledge when you travel via Airbnb."

At another location, we contacted our host because we were arriving at the rental late at night. The host made sure the fridge was stocked with milk for breakfast. Our son was very happy, which made us happy parents.

It also helps to spend time going through the rental with your host to make sure everything works as advertised. We created a **12-point checklist** (which we've included at the end of this chapter) so we don't forget anything. We typically go over this with our host when we first check into the Airbnb.

When you have a great host, you may want to ask them to connect you with a local babysitter so that you can go out and have some fun sans children. Some hosts will even offer babysitting themselves. Obviously, you want to go with your instincts here, and if you don't feel comfortable doing it, then don't do it. We used babysitters referred by Airbnb hosts in Rome, Bali, Lima, and Santiago. If you do take this route, **invite the babysitter** to come over and spend some time with you before you go.

(For more information on hiring a babysitter, see How To Find Babysitting Help When You Travel on the following page.)

How To Find Babysitting Help When You Travel

It can be extremely daunting to leave a child with someone you just met in a different country. If you're wondering how to use a babysitter during your next trip, the tips below may help you feel more at ease.

Here are a few ways to find babysitters while traveling:

◆ **Turn to your Airbnb host.** When you decide to stay at an Airbnb, you're placing a certain level of trust in your host. You can ask him or her if they have babysitters they recommend. In Peru, we used the babysitter our host uses regularly. In Rome, our host lived upstairs and had a teenage daughter who babysat for us.

◆ **Trust the hotel concierge.** Many resort hotel properties with concierges have "approved" lists of local babysitters who will come to the hotel. You can talk to the concierge about the level of experience of each sitter and how often they have babysat at the property.

◆ **Turn to websites.** Sites such as Care.com, www.sitters.co.uk, and Holiday-Sitters.com are filled with details on babysitters, in a style similar to TripAdvisor. You'll see photos, read reviews from other parents, learn about their levels of experience, and more.

Here are five ways to make the process easier and more comfortable for both you and your child:

1. **Meet with the sitter beforehand.** Set up a meeting at your hotel lobby, Airbnb, or a local coffee shop to interview your potential sitter, just as you would at home. If you don't leave the interview feeling completely comfortable with the sitter, don't proceed.

How To Find Babysitting Help When You Travel

2. **Have your sitter arrive ahead of time.** You don't want to just leave as soon as your sitter arrives. Spend half an hour together and help transition your child into spending time with a stranger. We would have the sitter arrive while Aarav was taking a bath, and we helped put him to bed with the sitter involved.

3. **Leave detailed instructions.** Make sure your sitter knows what to do (and not do) with your children. Also be clear on how you may be reached. (Tip: Make sure you have a good data plan on your phone so you can be reached at all times.)

4. **Don't book a sitter the night of your arrival.** It's difficult enough for a young child to adapt to new surroundings, so save hiring a sitter for the next day or two so that your child doesn't have too many changes all at once.

5. **Keep the time short and stay close.** Don't use a sitter for a full-day outing. Instead, use a sitter for an evening that gives you a private dinner or a chance to see a show—just a few hours, at most. And don't go too far. We stayed within 15 minutes of our Airbnb so we could get back quickly, if needed.

With strong recommendations and meeting with sitters beforehand, you can feel as confident and comfortable using a babysitter abroad as you would trying a new sitter at home.

To give you an idea of how special Airbnb truly is, here's a look at just some of our Airbnb stays from our trip around the world:

- ◆ **Bali.** This incredible rental sleeps up to seven guests and features three bedrooms, three bathrooms, a full kitchen, and a living room. But that's not all—we also had access to a private pool and housekeeper, which made for an ultra-luxurious experience. In all honesty, we didn't need that much space, but what an amazing way to experience beautiful Bali!

- ◆ **Rome.** This warm and inviting space sleeps up to eight guests and contains two bedrooms (four beds total) and two bathrooms. The host offers special personal touches from one-on-one cooking sessions featuring traditional Roman or Italian dishes to babysitting services. In fact, the host's daughter babysat Aarav for us (twice!) so that we could have some time to ourselves.

- ◆ **Zagreb.** This lovely Croatian apartment sleeps up to four guests and features two bedrooms, two bathrooms, a private balcony, and a beautiful view of the forest. Our Zagreb rental sticks out in our minds thanks to our thoughtful host: He took the time to provide a sign with our names on it and even provided a mini bar with drinks.

◆ **Lima.** This extremely affordable rental sleeps up to four guests and contains two bedrooms and two bathrooms. While staying here, we had the most amazing view of Kennedy Park and even scored another amazing babysitter recommendation.

◆ **Udaipur.** This modern, family-friendly space sleeps up to 10 guests and contains 5 bedrooms and 5 bathrooms. Located in the heart of the city next to the city palace, it features an open rooftop terrace and places you right in the middle of the city's action. We rented this Airbnb while traveling across India with our parents and found it both enjoyable and comfortable.

Visit our resources page at www.the2idiots.com/resources/ to get the direct links to these Airbnbs!

Safety

We're often asked whether Airbnb is really a safe option. This is where we'd point you back to the reviews. Generally, **reviewers will give you a good sense of whether or not they felt safe** in a particular part of town, whether they were comfortable walking at night, etc. That can be an invaluable resource to you as you make your travel plans. Your host will usually be able to help you navigate the area safely as well.

As long as you do your homework—such as reading reviews, planning appropriately—we think you'll agree with us that Airbnb is wonderfully flexible and accommodating.

You know we love Airbnbs but we have had a few negative experiences. Once our Airbnb host in Venice accused us of damaging her dishwasher (which stopped working during our stay) and wanted to claim a few hundred dollars from us. We went through the dispute resolution via Airbnb and didn't end up paying anything which was great. In another case, our host had to cancel the reservation on us last minute—Airbnb helped us find a new place plus gave us extra credits! Finally, our Airbnb in Seville the AC in the living room didn't work for the entire stay (in 90°F weather). This particular Airbnb only had a couple of reviews, and we learned the lesson to not take that chance again!

The 2 Idiots Airbnb 12-Point Check-In Checklist

☐ Ensure the home locks and the keys or codes work as expected.

☐ Ensure you have appropriate keys or codes to enter the building and parking garage.

☐ Connect to the Internet and make sure it's working by going to Google.

☐ Check the thermostat & AC/heater.

☐ Make sure the fridge is cold and working.

☐ Make sure the TV and TV channels are working as expected.

☐ If the place has a washing machine/dryer, check on them OR ensure there is a hanging rack.

☐ If the place has microwave, make sure it works.

☐ If the place has dishwasher, make sure it works.

☐ Check for all detergents (dish and clothes).

☐ Check for a broom and vacuum cleaner for cleaning.

☐ Check for dishes, cups, and silverware.

We have also made a printable and downloadable version of this checklist available exclusively to you at www.the2idiots.com/resources/.

Tales Of Tantrums And Many Cities

Tense moments, tiredness, hunger, and frustration all have the potential to lead to tantrums—especially when traveling by plane, car, bus, or train. To add more stress to the situation, you might be in a place where you cannot take your child out of the situation to handle the tantrum (like a plane). Because this is likely a new experience for your child, and maybe even for you, everything seems magnified when you are the parent. **This chapter is the epitome of "Empathize" from our Be F.L.E.X.I.B.L.E. philosophy.** As you embark, remember how important it is to practice patience with your partner, your child, and even other families. It helps to relieve the stress in those tense moments you're bound to experience.

Our philosophy is **travel tantrums are generally not the best time to teach your child a lesson.** Help your child move away from the tantrum and try to calm him/her as quickly as possible. Here are a few ideas that may help you through the process.

FIRST, **focus on your child.** Don't

AARAV THROWING A TANTRUM IN TALLINN, ESTONIA

worry so much about other people's feelings when your child is having a tantrum. By focusing on your child, you will be able to figure out what's causing the tantrum and calm your child much more quickly than stressing about the people around you. People are generally less frustrated than you imagine they are. Also, remember this is likely something new for your child; try to see things through his or her eyes. By doing this, you can help your child calm down more quickly.

"Focus on your child, not others."

AARAV THROWING A TANTRUM ON BONEYARD BEACH IN FLORIDA

SECOND, **be prepared.** How do you normally handle tantrums in tight situations? If you know there is a particular situation that sets your child off, try to avoid it. Make sure the batteries in your devices are charged. Have snacks ready. Let your child carry his favorite toy or blanket if it helps him or her deal with stress.

When Aarav throws a tantrum in a situation like this, we typically pick him up, hug him tight, and let him know it will be OK. We give him his milk (his favorite!). If that doesn't work, we we start improvising, perhaps by using M&Ms. For us, one of these three actions usually resolves the issue. Sometimes he's throwing a tantrum because he wants to see the gate numbers at the airport, or he wants to read some letters. If that's the case, we give him his five minutes or so to do what he wants, and he calms himself down.

THIRD, **work with your partner or traveling companion.** Be patient with each other and try to find a common ground on how to handle a tantrum. Nothing is worse than adding two screaming adults to an already screaming child. One approach is to take turns. We give each other breaks—especially on the longer flights. For instance, AJ would be on child duty for 20-30 minutes, and Natasha got to disappear into her headphones or whatever she wanted to do, then we swap. We actually used stopwatches to block off this time and found it to be a good approach. If you have more than one child you and your partner may choose to rotate from the more challenging child to the easier one—another way of making sure everyone gets a little break. There are many options here; just work together, plan it out before you go, and try to be patient with each other.

> "Be patient with your partner during a tantrum."

We were in Tallinn, Estonia, on a Scandinavian cruise, and, as usual, Aarav had found a square full of pigeons to chase. He would chase the birds until they all eventually perched on top of the buildings around us. He got super-upset and started screaming and crying because the birds wouldn't play with him. 😔

FOURTH, **ask for help** if you need it. If you need something, ask the flight attendant, train-car attendant, even other passengers. People are very willing to help, and someone else may have a new idea for dealing with the situation. On our travels we found people to be very kind and accommodating.

FINALLY, **have patience** for other people traveling with their kids. Offer help when you can and stay calm. The tantrum will end and everything will be OK. The good news is that tantrums eventually become great fodder for wedding toasts and horrifying potential dates.

We had to keep Aarav's stroller away in the coat-check area prior to a museum tour in St. Petersburg, Russia. On realizing this, Aarav had a complete meltdown and cried for several minutes straight 😧. A lady working in the coat-check area was screaming at us (in Russian) and gesturing at Aarav; she was obviously angry at a child's tantrum! AJ was mad and reacted strongly including yelling out a few choice words which we cannot print in this book. Eventually, Aarav calmed down and we carried him through the tour. Sometimes parents throw a tantrum too!

Tip: Try Our Calming Mantra

When we experience a mid-travel tantrum, we find that it helps to repeat our mantra: **"It's just a phase."** It may sound a bit simplistic, but saying those four little words out loud during a trying moment (or day) can bring some much-needed stress relief and peace.

As parents, we tend to get caught up in particularly difficult moments with our children and think "this" (whatever it may be) will last forever. But that simply isn't true. By reminding ourselves that it's just a phase, we've overcome some trying mid-travel moments, such as Aarav flipping out on our 70th flight or even refusing to eat a basic food such as bread while we were traveling.

ZZZZZZZZZ

Sleeping Nightmares

This is every parent's nightmare when traveling with children— their sleep routine will be disrupted, no one will get any sleep, and everyone will be miserable. This rings true especially when you know you'll be crossing time zones. From our experience, **children are**

AARAV ASLEEP DURING OUR WATER SAFARI AT CHOBE NATIONAL PARK, BOTSWANA

very adaptable, and worrying about their sleep schedule shouldn't keep you from traveling. Yes, you may have some trying times, but overall, things will likely go more smoothly than you thought. Here are a few tips we've learned along the way.

....

Sleeping arrangements

If you are a parent that co-sleeps with your child, you can skip this section.

For parents whose children sleep in their own bed and/or rooms (including us), this is an important subject to tackle prior to travel.

First, let's talk about our **sleeping checklist**. The first thing you need is a travel bassinet (for infants) or a travel crib (for toddlers or older). For our big trip, we used the Guava Lotus Travel Crib, and we highly recommend it. The Guava Crib is super-light to travel with (we have carried it on the plane), easy to set up and provides plenty of space for your child (get more information on this travel crib and other recommended travel bassinets or travel cribs on our blog). Airbnb hosts and hotels can also provide a crib at your destination so you have to decide if carrying another piece of luggage around is worth it (it was for us while we traveled the world!). We also carry a travel baby monitor and have downloaded an app (Relax Melodies) to our phones and iPad to provide white noise.

Now let's talk about the **room situation**. If your child sleeps in their own room at home it's best to get them a separate room during your travels. Airbnb is the easiest solution and we usually try to book two-bedroom apartments for our travels. Set up the crib in this separate room as soon as you can and reinforce with your child that this is his/her room. With a one-bedroom, just set up the crib in the corner of the room with a clear path for you to get to your bed and the bathroom. Put your child to sleep in the room and have a mini-date night in the living room while your child is falling asleep. Aarav is a pretty sound sleeper, and we can usually get back into the room later without disturbing him. In this scenario, before you put your kids to sleep for the night, prepare for bed yourselves—wash up, brush your

teeth, and change into pajamas—so you don't wake them later.
Because it's a new environment, the first night might be the hardest for your child. We try to make sure Aarav is super-tired on the first night so he goes to sleep immediately, but that's not a given. There have been times he won't fall asleep, and after numerous attempts, we let him sleep with us on the first night. While this might be scary to parents who worry about sleeping habits, don't worry, the second night is very different. By then, Aarav has typically adjusted to time zone changes and is more comfortable in his new environment giving everyone a good night's sleep.

One exception: If we are in a hotel room just for one overnight stay (e.g., when we want to fly out of a city the next day), we typically don't bother setting up a crib or trying to keep a sleep schedule. We just have him sleep in the bed with us for that night and wake up together. On the rare occasion we book a hotel room for multiple nights, we try to book a suite and use the same strategies as with the one-bedroom apartment above.

Now that he is older (approximately three and a half), he will sleep on a pull-out bed or even a normal-size bed. We create a pillow fort around him under the sheets to prevent any falls, and that has worked pretty well for us.

· ·

Sleeping on a plane

"Book a late flight for long journeys."

Whether you're traveling to another state or another country in another time zone, you're going to be faced with being cooped up for long amounts of time. It can be tough to keep your kids entertained in such a confined space, so getting them to sleep during the trip can be a life-saver. **If you know the trip will be long, plan for an overnight or late-night flight.** Your child will already be tired. They'll fall asleep during the flight and hopefully sleep until you arrive at your destination. This also allows you to catch some sleep, and you're not stressed out trying to entertain and manage your child.

AARAV SLEEPING ON AIR INDIA FLIGHT FROM TOKYO TO NEW DELHI

Time zones and jet lag

"Let your child sleep around your vacation schedule—not the other way around."

Crossing time zones keeps a lot of parents from traveling to countries they're yearning to see. If it's 7 p.m. in the eastern US (when your child might typically go to bed), it's already 1 a.m. in Spain or 4:30 a.m. in India. That is sure to throw a kink in things, right? Not necessarily.

For instance, in Spain, the culture is much different. People often don't start eating dinner until 8 or 9 p.m. By the time dinner is over, you're back at your hotel, and your child has had their time to unwind, it may be around 1 a.m., which is close to their bedtime in the US anyway. Not much adjusting to do. And by allowing them to stay up later, they can taste the local cuisine and not be stuck eating McDonald's or snack food because they're going to bed before dinner is served.

When we went to Iceland, we had a four-hour time change, and dinner time was around 7 p.m., so we wanted our son to go to bed soon after. However, it would still be pretty early in the US, so we took steps to help him adjust. A day or two before traveling, we would wake Aarav up two or three hours earlier than normal and have him go to bed earlier that night. This helped with the transition.

If it is a major time change and you can't adjust beforehand—like when we flew from Dubai to Beijing—your best bet is to improvise and simply **go with the flow.** When we arrived in Beijing, it was around midnight, but it was only 8 p.m. in Dubai where we had just been. Our son was not tired yet, because he was used to going to bed in another three or four hours. We eventually went to bed at 4 a.m. (yes, really). In this situation, we suggest you don't try to force your child to go to sleep. You'll be frustrated, they'll be frustrated, and it rarely works out. Instead, stay up and go to bed when they tire. **Within a day or two, you will all adjust.**

East vs. West

How you deal with time zone changes really depends on the arrival time at your destination, and the ability to transition easily depends on whether you travel east or west. As a general rule of thumb, **we have found traveling east to be more difficult than traveling west.** Traveling east means you can often end up in the situation such as the one we describe above in traveling from Dubai to Beijing. While traveling east, spend more time on planning for the time zone change and be ready to be super-flexible when you arrive at your destination. You will often have to stay up late into the night since there is a possibility your kids won't be tired enough. This is often made worse due to the nature of travel and kids not having a way to burn a lot of energy on a plane ride.

Some strategies that have worked for us are:

1. **Wake your kids up earlier** than usual a day or two before traveling (as in the Iceland example above).

2. **Don't let your children take their scheduled afternoon naps,** so they are more exhausted at the destination.

3. **Wake up your child at an earlier time the next day,** regardless of how long he/she sleeps at night. For example in Beijing, we went to sleep at 4 a.m. the first night, but we woke up at 11 a.m. the next day—so just seven hours of sleep for the little one. Then we went to sleep around midnight that night. By the next morning, we had mostly adjusted to the jet lag!

We also recommend you don't book any early-morning activities or tours the morning after you travel east. It might be hard to get up yourself, let alone wake up your kids.

Traveling west is usually easier because you generally get to your destination at a decent time. However, since it's typically much later at the original destination, the key is to keep your kids awake late enough so they can get a good night's sleep. Hopefully they won't wake up at an abominably early hour. You want to typically do the reverse of traveling east, and here are some strategies you can use.

1. **Let your kids sleep in** a day or two before traveling and go to sleep later than you generally do.

2. **Ensure your children take their scheduled naps,** so they are awake and active when you get to your destination.

3. **Keep them up** by taking them to a movie, to the park, or by doing whatever activities they get excited about.

If your kids falls asleep earlier than you want them to, **just go with the flow,** and prepare for them to wake up earlier the next morning. That next evening, extend it a couple of hours later, and in a couple of days, you will all have beaten the jet lag!

Afternoon naps

If you take a break for a few hours in the middle of the day for an afternoon nap, it can be very limiting, and you miss out on a lot. If your child is tired, they will sleep wherever they are. Bring a stroller so they have somewhere comfortable to sleep, and you can give your arms a break. For very young children, you can use a baby carrier if that is more comfortable and convenient.

Regardless of your child's nap schedule, we encourage you to stick with your travel plans for the day and do your sightseeing. **No matter how close or far you are traveling, have that stroller or carrier handy.** Our son fell asleep at the Vatican, Victoria Falls, and even surrounded by kangaroos in Australia. Don't interrupt your plans to go back to the hotel and miss out on what you want to do; let them sleep wherever you are.

AARAV ASLEEP AT THE IGUANA PARK IN GUAYAQUIL, ECUADOR

Readjusting at home

It may take a day or two, but your child will get back to their normal routine pretty quickly. In the meantime, **be flexible and adjust** your schedule a bit until things are back on track.

....

Don't let sleep stop you

Don't let worrying about your child's sleep schedule keep you from traveling. Be flexible. Plan ahead when possible. Go with the flow and **don't stress out.** Your child will adjust and so will you.

When we flew to Iceland, Aarav hadn't adjusted to the time change. We did his nighttime routine and put him in his crib, but he just wouldn't sleep. It was still early in the US and he wasn't having it. After many failed attempts, we took him out of the crib and let him play for a couple of hours until he was completely exhausted. He quickly adjusted after that, and we had a well-rested, happy toddler.

Food Diaries

Food is always a concern for parents, especially when traveling out of the country. Will the food suit your child's tastes? Is the water safe to drink? Will your child feel sick from a change to their usual menu?

For starters, **make sure you carry food with you as a part of your packing strategy** (see *Pack Like Mary Poppins*). We pack our son's favorite foods in our check-in luggage and some snacks in our carry-on bags (we typically only pack commercially packaged foods since some countries have very strict rules, especially regarding fresh foods, meats, and anything not commercially packaged.)

NATASHA ENJOYING A FABULOUS MEAL ON OUR CRUISE STOP IN KOTOR, MONTENEGRO

The biggest thing we've learned is to go with the flow in terms of your child's hunger. When you travel, there is no need to stick to an eating schedule—unless your child has specific medical needs.

We adjusted our son's eating schedule to follow his nap and bed-time routine. For example, if he seemed sleepy before a planned activity, we would feed him before going out. This way, he was full before his nap and would sleep longer, making him a much happier traveling companion.

Also, *always* feed your child before going on tours, if you can. We made this mistake a few times early in our traveling adventure. We would be on a tour, and he would get hungry and cranky. That would detract from the experience because we needed to take care of his needs midway. Learn from our mistake and feed your child before leaving your accommodations.

Restaurants in most places have a small portion or kids menu. Just ask before you are seated. They usually have simpler foods for kids' undeveloped taste buds. If the menu has nothing that your child would like, the easiest way to enjoy yourselves is to **feed your child before you go to the restaurant.** If that's not possible, have enough snacks with you that will make up for a meal. We carried pistachios, chips, and fruit/granola bars, and there were several times when he just ate chips for dinner. We enjoyed our meal and so did he. Another good option is to ask for bread since kids will typically eat that.

We also recommend to "Embrace Technology" and use devices when going to restaurants; This will help your child sit in one place for a longer period of time. While he was distracted (learning!), we used it as an opportunity to expand his food palate and try new things. If he didn't like it, he just spit it out, but he tried all kinds of foods.

"Cut yourself some slack. Give your child a device so you can enjoy a meal together."

Food safety while traveling (especially internationally) can be a big concern. In some countries you can't drink the tap water or eat any street vendor foods. To keep our son safe from potential bacteria, we would boil the milk in certain countries and use bottled water whenever we needed to. We were cautious around uncooked foods—raw vegetables, greens, and fruits, and obviously raw meats—especially in countries with concern regarding their water quality. We just made sure we ate fully-cooked food and we had no issues.

At some eateries, **we would feed Aarav with our hands, and we believe that helped keep him from getting sick.** He was free to play around and put his hands everywhere, but those hands didn't go on foods he was going to eat. If your child has to eat with his/her hands, make sure you wash and use hand sanitizer before eating.

If you aren't sure about the food and water situation in a particular country, ask your tour guide, Airbnb host, hotel concierge, and—the easiest—Google. For example, just search, "Is tap water safe to drink in Mumbai?"

"Be careful consuming raw foods and tap water when traveling internationally."

You can enjoy exotic foods and local cuisine as long as you take some basic precautions. Trying new foods is one of our favorite parts of traveling to new places.

AMAZING FOOD PLATTER IN LIMA, PERU

After a long train ride from Seville to Barcelona, we looked around for places to eat. We found a great Mediterranean shawarma shop and assumed Aarav would eat the chicken as he usually does, but he had other plans. We couldn't coax him into eating anything, so his meal was chips and pistachios that night. Hey, nuts count as protein right?

5 Tips To Save Money on Food

Eating out can get pretty costly, and it can be difficult to stay on budget, especially when visiting different countries. Here are some of our tips to keep your food costs in check:

1. **Book an Airbnb or a hotel room with a kitchenette.** We typically cooked breakfast every day and often had lunch at our Airbnb, and then we went out to dinner to enjoy the local cuisine and the nightlife. This saved us a ton of money; instead of spending on three daily meals (times three!) we only had one meal out each day. If you prefer a hotel to an Airbnb, look for hotel rooms with a refrigerator, microwave, and stove top.

2. **Get a quick meal for your children.** Before dining at a high-end restaurant, stop in a local quick-service restaurant (even if it is McDonald's). Children don't care for expensive meals, so allowing them to eat a cheap meal before you go to a restaurant will save you money. (It's also helpful in the event children don't like the local cuisine; finding our son chicken nuggets rather than a more expensive meal in China, for example, could help him eat what he liked.)

5 Tips To Save Money on Food

3. **Order half portions.** Kids' menus are found across America, but when traveling the world, they aren't as common. Simply request a half-portion of a meal for your child, which costs half the price. Many restaurants are willing to do this for customers, especially pint-sized ones. (This could backfire on you, though. In Zagreb, Croatia, Aarav decided he wanted our kebabs, and we had to give him our food and eat his more "bland" meal!) If you cannot get a half order, share some of your adult meals with your children.

4. **Have a picnic in a park.** Even if you don't have a kitchen where you are staying, you should always shop a local market and enjoy a picnic lunch in a park, which also gives your a child a chance to play. For example, we love Central Park in New York; it's one of our favorite parks and is a great place for picnics—you're in the middle of a huge city and wouldn't know it.

5. **Look for children's deals.** Many hotels provide discounted, if not free, meals for kids under 12. They also may offer free breakfasts for the entire family. Look for restaurants that offer specials, and turn to discount sites, including Groupon and Living Social, both available around the world, which can score you discounts on dining out in the destinations you are visiting.

Keeping The Doctor Away

Our family spent nine months traveling around the world, visiting six continents and 31 countries with our two-year-old son. Two-year-olds often get sick within a nine-month period at home, especially when exposed to lots of kids in daycare, so of course, he got sick while we were on the road. We learned how to care for our ill child while traveling, and although we are not doctors, we do have some tips for other parents who find their child under the weather when traveling.

Disclaimer: Any suggestions here are not meant to take the place of professional advice. Please consult a doctor if you are worried about your child's well-being.

Talk to your doctor

Before traveling to exotic locations with your child, visit your pediatrician and make sure there are **no health concerns** for countries you are planning to visit. This is also an opportunity to get any inoculations your child may need *(don't forget to visit your own doctor to get yours)*. This appointment should take place at least a month before you travel.

Letting your doctor know about your travels may also have other benefits. If your child gets sick while traveling, and you need your doctor to fill a prescription for you, he/she will already be prepared to help. Your doctor is also likely to have travel tips for you and your kid(s) on how to avoid and handle illness in different locations. **Listen to your doctor's advice and concerns.** She/he knows your child's medical history and will be able to offer pinpointed advice for your child. For our travels, our son needed yellow fever vaccinations prior to traveling to Africa and South America and malaria pills (crushed up in his orange juice) for Africa.

"Be proactive with sickness."

Pack a medicine bag

Travel with essential medicines. Visiting a pharmacy and buying over-the-counter medications can be unnerving, especially in a foreign country. You may not be able to connect with the right words for the medicine you need or may be uncomfortable purchasing medicine with labels in another language. See our list in *Pack Like Mary Poppins* for more details.

Plan ahead for special circumstances

Sometimes you'll know ahead of time if a special situation or circumstance can arise that will impact your child's health. One of the most concerning circumstances is if your child has any food allergies—especially if you're traveling to foreign countries. The good news is that we have some helpful advice to help you plan ahead for such situations. If you're concerned about your child encountering specific foods that may cause severe reactions, consider the following:

Make your own meals. If you're staying at an Airbnb rental, you'll likely have access to a kitchen. Preparing your child's meals can help offset the likelihood that he or she will come into contact with an offending food because you'll have complete control over all of the ingredients in their meals.

Carry an Epipen. If your child has severe food allergies, you never want to leave home without this life-saving medication. Make sure you have it with you at all times.

Use Google Translate. If you're at a restaurant and you don't recognize some of the ingredients in a dish, Google Translate can be a great tool to make sure your child steers clear of any allergens. Be sure to download the offline dictionary as well so you can translate the menu even when WiFi isn't available.

Know the location of the nearest doctor. For extreme situations, it's always a good idea to know where the closest hospital or pediatrician is located. Likewise, if you're particularly concerned about your child encountering a life-threatening ingredient in their food, it's probably best to avoid activities that require remote locations, such as safaris.

Practice prevention

Keep germs at bay by washing your hands often. When traveling, you are exposing yourself and your child to lots of new germs. Carry antibacterial wipes to stay clean and make sure you wipe your child's hands frequently. Kids love to touch everything, and rather than not allowing them to explore, just help them stay clean. **We would often feed our son with our hands if we were worried about what he had been touching.** Be diligent about using mosquito repellent when needed to ward off dangerous viruses found in some countries.

Get lots of rest. When you run yourself ragged, you all increase your chance of getting sick. When we get tired, we sometimes let certain things slide a little. That little slip might be your undoing. If your child does get sick, make sure they take lots of naps and get to bed early. Sleep will help them get better faster.

Don't panic

Don't let one cough or sneeze freak you out. Most kids with a cold can still manage and can get their rest sleeping in their stroller, well bundled. Treat a cold as you would at home. Use over-the-counter-medications, if available, and keep an eye on your child to make sure things don't escalate. Remember, **keep your child well hydrated** when sick or well— lots of water is important when traveling. Contact your doctor if your child is prone to rapid advancement of illness.

Be sure to **travel with a thermometer** so you can check for a fever if your child gets sick. A low-grade fever may be something you can manage with over-the-counter medication, but if it gets into the danger zone for your child, go to the nearest hospital or clinic.

• •

Cancel your plans

If your child has a slight fever or is throwing up, it's best to **cancel your plans for the day.** Stay at your hotel or Airbnb and let your child rest in comfort. One parent can get food from a local grocery while the other stays with the child. If it is a travel day, by plane especially, you need to gauge the illness to determine whether you should push on or cancel your plans. It can be risky to travel and not be close to a doctor or hospital as would be the case on a ten-hour flight.

"Be ready to adjust your travel plans if your child is sick."

Travel plans can always be adjusted. It might be a pain, but it's better than something terrible happening to your child.

On our son's first trip to Dubai, he wound up with a high fever. We had to cancel our travel plans to the beach. We took him to the doctor, who was worried about him getting tuberculosis (so scary!). She strongly recommended we stay at home, which we did, and gave us appropriate medication. In a couple of days, he was better. We missed the beach, but we took care of our son, which was way more important anyway.

· ·

Be patient

When your child gets sick, he'll need some **extra loving.** Don't get upset if whining increases as children are likely to be super-cranky and maybe even a bit annoying when they are sick, much like adults. With extra coddling and patience, it will be easier to manage. If your child gets sick, put yourself in their shoes, imagine what you would need to feel better, and offer the same to your child. They will get better soon and you can complete your travels.

· ·

Don't let fear stop you

No one wants to get sick when on vacation, but it does happen. **Be prepared** for kinks in your travel plans, but **don't let fear of illness stop you from taking a trip with your young child.** For us, our trip was priceless. We grew closer, created incredible memories, and are eager to travel together again, even if we get sick.

We have had days where we felt a little under the weather, but the person who felt the most sick during our trip was AJ. We were in Mumbai, India, and I (AJ) had a fever, but I obviously (stupidly) continued to work out and decided to have a night out with our friends. Needless to say, fever and alcohol don't mix well. My claim to fame is that I terrified my friends and the hip folks of Mumbai by fainting at a happening restaurant on a Thursday night. I was completely fine, just dehydrated. But in retrospect, I should have listened to my body and stayed in that evening.

Saving Private Poopers

Parents have many reservations about traveling with young children, mostly imagining it will be too difficult to do. But what happens when your child is also toilet training? Considering potty training takes six months or longer to get through before accidents stop, it's difficult enough not traveling while your child is potty training. However, you may worry that it will be more trouble than it's worth or that travel will cause your child to revert back to diapers.

Let's begin with the basics: **yes, potty training while traveling will be hard.** Yes, there will be accidents. Yes, it will be frustrating. However, introducing your child to using different toilets and learning to cope with change will make your child more adaptable and resilient.

"Traveling while toilet training will make your child more adaptable and resilient."

We'll admit that AJ found potty training super-frustrating and **one of the hardest things he's had to do as a parent.** So, the following is mostly advice from Natasha who handled it like a champ.

1. Don't start potty training while you are traveling. It's much too difficult to begin a routine while you are on the road. Start a minimum of two weeks before your trip—longer, if you can.

2. Prepare mentally. Understand things will not go as well as you hope; sometimes your child won't want to go to the bathroom in a strange place. There may be screaming and shouting (by your child, but if you end up in this state with him/her, we won't judge). Go into this knowing it will be hard, and remember, just like everything else in travel, some things won't be easy, but it will be worth it in the end.

3. When going to the airport, put your child in a pull-up. With long lines at check-in and security, as well as flight delays, you won't have the control you need to properly potty train. Wearing a pull-up will take away some of the stress. We also put our child in pull-ups whenever we left the hotel and then back into his underwear at the hotel. While some feel reverting to pull-ups will make a child forget potty training, you can treat them like regular underwear, and if there is an accident, you avoid all the cleanup.

4. Use the bathroom as often as you can. Before you leave the house, after your check-in, after you are through security, and on the plane, try going to the bathroom. In fact, every time you leave the hotel or arrive at an attraction, go to the bathroom first. Make it your No. 1 Mom Rule: no one leaves without going to the bathroom. Additionally having your child try different bathrooms will get them more accustomed to using strange toilets and help make them better travelers. This is also a great reason to have your child wash their hands more frequently to avoid germs.

"No. 1 Mom Rule: no one leaves without going to the bathroom."

5. Bring a portable potty seat that fits into your carry-on. This can become a familiar seat for your child to use, no matter the bathroom.

6. Pack a potty-prepared bag. In it we carry an extra set of clothes, in case of an accident (there will be accidents), plastic bags to hold soiled clothing, flushable wipes to clean up, and pull-ups or other nighttime system you are using for sleep.

7. Don't panic when there is an accident. Accidents will happen. Having your bag for a quick cleanup can help calm your child. Don't punish your child for making a potty-training mistake. Reassure your son or daughter that it's okay, and they can try again.

8. If you are incentivizing potty training, bring those incentives with you as well. For us, it is M&Ms, but whatever it is you are using to reward positive bathroom experiences, bring those to continue the training.

Even at home, kids will go back and forth on their toilet training, and it's normal. Don't let potty training stop you from taking a trip with your child. Remember, you are building long-term adaptability and incredible memories.

We were stuck on an active runway for a long time, and Aarav, who was early in his toilet training, needed to use the bathroom. We used the button to call the flight attendant and pleaded to let us take him to the bathroom, to which he agreed. Disaster averted! *phew*

How To Take Your Kids Anywhere!

Many parents may think the things you would do as a couple when you travel cannot be done anymore because you have children. **Based on "Xperience" from Be F.L.E.X.I.B.L.E., this chapter will encourage you to create amazing memories as a family and simply enjoy the journey ahead.**

We've gone on a safari, visited wineries and distilleries, taken a helicopter ride, and gone snorkeling, all with our two-year-old son accompanying us. You can do the things you want to do. **Having children shouldn't stop you from doing the things you love.** Here, in this chapter, we provide some tips to help you get through the following nine unique situations while traveling with kids.

- Walking Tours
- Group Bus Tours
- Museums
- Shows
- Wine and Distillery Tours
- Cable Cars
- Snorkeling
- Helicopter Tours
- Safaris

"You don't have to give up fun experiences just because you have kids."

For every tour, there are 5 things you should always be sure to do before you go:

1. Bring distractions. Never attempt a tour without all of your child's favorite things. Bring your child's toy bag and have his or her favorite books, toys and snacks in it. Also, for the rare occasions those distractions don't work, make sure you have the big guns: educational apps and emergency chocolate.

2. Get your travel stroller. If you are traveling through a museum where you need to prevent your children from touching art or running around, stroller time keeps control. Other times, places may be crowded and a stroller can make it easier to maneuver through crowds and not lose your child. Of course, strollers are also great when your child needs a nap and you're still out exploring.

PICTURE OF NATASHA PUSHING AARAV ON OUR WALKING TOUR IN ST. AUGUSTINE, FL

3. Go potty. Before you start any tour make sure you have changed your children's diapers and put on a fresh one or have had your children go to the bathroom.

4. Prevent "hangry". Like the Snickers commercials—your children aren't themselves when they get hungry. A hungry child can quickly become a cranky child, so be sure to feed your children before you go on a tour, and bring snacks and milk with you, just in case.

5. Draw straws. Decide before you go which parent will sit out of a tour with children, and be prepared for it to happen. You don't want to be arguing over who should leave when your children are having a tantrum.

Walking Tours

It took us a few months during our nine-month trip around the world with our two-year-old son to brave a walking tour with him. We had been too nervous to try a walking tour, but after taking our first tour—and surviving—we discovered we had been missing out. From that moment on, at practically every new city we visited, from Buenos Aires to Rome to Lima to Barcelona, we signed up for walking tours with our son.

"Be ready to take turns."

To us, **walking tours are a must because they provide a true local's perspective on a city,** as well as insights we may have missed if exploring on our own. Most of the tours we discovered were free, as well, led by passionate guides with attention for detail who were often students of art, architecture, and history.

Not all of our tours went without a hitch. In Venice, we learned the hard way that carrying a stroller up and down more than 30 bridges crossing the city's canals was quite a workout. In Buenos Aires, our optimism at joining a three-hour tour didn't match our son's desire to stay awake the entire time, demanding attention, toys, food, and even a poopy diaper change on the street. However, most of our tours—and we have taken more than a dozen—went quite well.

In addition to the universal tips mentioned above, here are specific tips for a walking tour:

◆ **Tour during naptimes.** Most tours are offered in the morning, afternoon, and nighttime, but we quickly learned the afternoon tours were best for our son. We would spend our morning at parks and being quite active, feed our son lunch, and then put him in his stroller and walk to the tour. By the time our tours would begin, he would be asleep for his afternoon nap, typically sleeping through the entire 1.5- to 2-hour tours.

◆ **Bring your stroller, no matter what.** We've said this once, we say it again: **Do not attempt a walking tour without a stroller—even** on cobbled and small streets of Europe and even if guides tell you to leave the stroller. Not only does your stroller foster naptime, it can also keep your child contained and allow you to provide distractions during your walk. We took a tour of the Colosseum and Palatine Hill in Rome that quickly became a disaster. The reason? We didn't bring our stroller because the guide said they wouldn't be allowed (not true!). That was the only tour we had to leave early because it became too hard to manage Aarav without one. Never again!

◆ **Divide and conquer.** At times when your child is too antsy for the tour, or is throwing a tantrum, have one parent continue with the tour while the other stays back to get things under control. It's okay to divide and conquer; just agree on who will be the "designated parent" that day. We used to do it in 30-minute increments and then switch. Your partner can text you a location for meeting up, and fill you in on what you missed. Be sure you have a good data plan for your phone, just in case you get lost. Also, ask the guide where they are heading to next, so you can stay back and catch up.

◆ **Set them free.** Talk to your tour guide before you begin to find out where may be longer stops to allow your child to climb out of the stroller to play. Some stops can be 10 to 15 minutes long, and can give your child a break.

One of the toughest free walking tours we took was in Argentina., It was a 3-hour tour, which is a long time (we typically prefer tours that are 90 minutes to 2 hours)! We had planned for Aarav to sleep, which he didn't, and so we quickly ran out of milk. AJ had to rush into a grocery store and get additional milk. And then, in the middle of the tour, Aarav pooped. With no bathroom in sight, AJ had to change his diaper literally on the side of the street while the group moved on, so he had to rush to catch up to Natasha. It was a hard tour but we got to see beautiful Buenos Aires and have great stories to tell Aarav when he is older.

Group Bus Tours

We generally dislike group bus tours, but sometimes there is no way around it. We have taken bus tours along the Amalfi Coast in Italy, in Scandinavia, Thailand, Vietnam, and St. Petersburg. Even though we tend to avoid bus tours, sometimes they offer exclusive access and are the only way to see everything in a short period of time, or because they are cheaper than a private tour. We generally prefer private tours for the flexibility; on a group bus tour, there is almost none. (Learn how to book the best private tours on our blog with our article, Finding The Best Private Tours When You Travel. 🗗) But when you can't avoid one, here are some tips.

◆ **Sit in the back.** There is more space in the back, and you can play games and not disturb other passengers. Plus, if the bus has a bathroom, it will be in the back.

◆ **Do what you want to do.** Our bus tour in Bangkok stopped at a glass-making facility that was probably paying the tour company to stop there and was essentially a tourist trap, while across the street a festival was going on with a play area for kids. We chose not to go into the facility and went to the festival instead. Be mindful of the time so you don't delay or miss the bus, but do not feel you have to do everything the guide is doing at each stop.

◆ **Be the last to enter and leave.** Be the last to get on and off the bus to make it easier for you, as well as the other passengers.

◆ **Communicate with your guide.** Let them know you need stop for a diaper change or if there is something you need. Generally, guides will understand and will help you. Also, be sure to have the cell phone number of your guide in case something goes wrong.

◆ **Return to the bus at least five minutes early.** If you are given time to explore a certain stop on your own, be back at the bus before the time given to you by your guide.

AMAZING VIEW OF POSITANO FROM OUR BUS TOUR THROUGH THE AMALFI COAST

Our cruise ship stopped in Naples and we booked a group tour to go all the way to Positano along the Amalfi coast. We had to leave around 8 a.m. so it could cover all the sights and sounds and make it back in time. We woke up around 6:30 a.m. that day and had to wake up Aarav before his regular schedule. While he was a little cranky waking up early, he went to sleep on the bus ride to our first stop and caught up on his sleep. This was one of the best tours we had taken. We saw the charming city of Sorrento, amazing Pompeii ruins, and the beautiful Amalfi coast. Plus, the driver and the guide were super kid-friendly. Moral of the story is that kids adapt no matter what the situation.

Museums

We've been to museums all over the world, including some fun museums like the Miniatur Wunderland in Hamburg, Germany, or the Automobile and Fashion Museum in Malaga, Spain. We have also been to art museums, science museums, and history museums.

When you are visiting the more serious museums where your children cannot touch anything, here are a few tips.

◆ **Use your stroller.** It can be difficult to manage children in a crowded museum following a tour. Keep your children buckled into a stroller, which can also keep them from touching anything. Many tours will say it's not

"No. 1 Dad Rule: Get your stroller no matter what."

wise to take a stroller. **Ignore them.** Museums are handicap accessible and you will be able to manage with a stroller. Never listen to a guide who tells you cannot manage a stroller in a museum; you can and you should! Ignore anyone telling you not to use a stroller! (Yes, we are repeating this because this is too important!)

◆ **Have your distractions.** If your young children will get bored at a museum, have an arsenal of distractions. Have books, electronics, and things to occupy your child's attention.

◆ **Visit the gardens prior.** Many museums have gardens and we found taking our son to play in the gardens before we started the tour helped him get his energy out before we did the "boring" stuff.

THE INCREDIBLE MINIATUR WUNDERLAND MUSEUM IN HAMBURG

When we toured Vatican City's museums, it was so unbelievably crowded, we wouldn't have been able to keep track of Aarav, so we kept him in his stroller. With so many people, it feels like you are cattle moving through the different rooms so having Aarav in the stroller was easier and helped us push through crowds. He eventually fell asleep, which meant we ended up having to carry him up and down 800 stairs throughout the museum. It was difficult, but we joke that we got a good workout that day. It was also good that he was asleep when we entered the Sistine Chapel, where the security staff was barking at everyone to keep quiet.

Shows

Sometimes, travel takes you to a place where the entertainment shouldn't be missed. What would Las Vegas, New York, or even a cruise be without attempting to see at least one show? Every time we go to a show, we get nervous as to how we are going to manage our son. Yet, we don't want to miss out. It takes some strategic planning to see a show your children wouldn't be interested in seeing.

◆ **Choose an appropriate show.** We would never take our son to see an opera or where being quiet is very important. If a show is medium- to high-energy, dancing, singing, loud, or kid-friendly, then yes, those are the shows for you.

◆ **Book a show at bedtime or naptime.** If a show is later in the evening, have dinner, change your children into pajamas, put them into the stroller, and walk around before the show to try to get them to fall asleep. We would put noise-canceling headphones on our son during shows, as well, to help him sleep.

◆ **Sit along the aisle in the back of the theater.** Just in case we need a fast getaway, we always sit in the back in an aisle seat so we can leave without disturbing others. (Or at the corner of a table closest to the door, if it is table seating.)

◆ **Be prepared to leave.** Like many tours, sometimes it won't go smoothly and you'll have to take your children out of the show. Sometimes you have to make the sacrifice; decide who will be the one to leave **before the show starts.**

During our Scandinavian cruise, we decided to see a violinist play—what could go wrong? Aarav had not yet fallen asleep before the show began, and again, we innocently thought the music would soothe him. When the violinist spoke, he would drift off, but when she played, oh boy! She would start soft and then the music would grow louder and louder. While it was beautiful, it would wake Aarav up and he would scream. Then she would speak again and he'd fall back asleep. We tried giving him milk to soothe him, but it didn't work. After a couple of cycles of this, AJ had to leave the show and ended up watching it from the back entrance with Aarav finally asleep in his stroller, away from the noise. At least Natasha enjoyed a great show!

Wine and Distillery Tours

This may sound like a crazy thing we do. People may say, "I can't believe you go on wine or distillery tours with kids." But who best to need wine and spirits than a parent?

We find that wine and distillery tours are actually some of the easiest and most kid-friendly tours we have done. We have done tours in South Africa, Mendoza, California, and Florida just to name a few—and they are super fun for kids. The great thing about these tours is that they are often outdoors and kids can literally run around. Many places we visited, including Cape Town, South Africa, have a lot of cool things for kids, including chalkboards to color on, kids' menus, and play areas.

ENJOYING THE CAYMAN SPIRITS COMPANY DISTILLERY TOUR IN GRAND CAYMAN

◆ **Wear comfortable shoes.** You could be walking a lot around a vineyard or distillery, so wear comfortable, closed-toe shoes to explore.

◆ **Bring insect repellent.** You'll be outside, often near grapes and foods that attract bugs. Be prepared with bug spray.

◆ **Use your travel stroller.** While there is ample room to run during the outdoor portion of a tour, when you enter the plant or winery, it's best to put your children in a stroller. Some passages will be narrow and there are working elements of the processing facility that your children shouldn't touch or get too close to. Use their bag of toys and electronics during this portion to distract them.

In Grand Cayman, we went on a distillery tour where a group of young women celebrating a birthday getaway were a part of our tour. It turned out they were all nannies and love children! Aarav was the only kid on the tour and they played with him and entertained him the entire tour! He had so much fun having all of the attention and people to play with, and, of course, they made it easier for us to sample different vodkas. So, we had a blast, too!

Cable Cars

Every now and then, you may have to take a cable car to get to a destination. We've been on cable cars in Greece, in Switzerland, China, and Spain. When Natasha was a child, she was so afraid of cable cars that no one in her family could go on a cable car. Now, she has taken numerous cable car rides (still not easy for her) in an attempt not to miss anything. While those with a fear of heights may struggle with a cable car ride, kids absolutely love them, and you can get to some amazing places, such as the Great Wall of China or Santorini.

NATASHA SCARED OF THE CABLE CAR RIDE IN SANTORINI

- ◆ **Divide and conquer.** Getting on a cable car with a ton of people in line can be nerve-wracking, especially when it is a moving cable car that doesn't stop for you to board. Have one parent handle the gear while the other handles your children.

- ◆ **Get a good spot.** If there are too many people ahead of you in line and you're going to be jammed, wait for the next one and get to the first in line. You want to be able to get a seat, if one is available, or have space by a window so you can show your children fun things they are seeing.

Natasha has a horrible fear of cable cars and heights. When she was a child, she would scream so much, her family never went on cable cars. Now, for the sake of our travels, she manages to get through them in order to see the cool sites. But she still hates the journey. Getting from the port to the top of Santorini requires climbing 587 steps up the mountain or taking a cable car that will make the 720-feet climb. With a toddler in tow, we had to take the cable car. That 720 feet is long, so the cars move fast, and when the wind hits, the cars sway. Not fun for Natasha! Not only did AJ have to care for Aarav, he also had to keep Natasha calm. It was definitely not a pleasant experience for her, but Natasha would do it all over to see Santorini again!

Snorkeling

We love snorkeling because it's a great way to see underwater wildlife with your family. When people hear we have taken Aarav snorkeling, they think we literally took him snorkeling, which is not possible, he's too young. He has, however, accompanied us on several snorkeling tours, including in the Galapagos, Bali, the Great Barrier reef, and Grand Cayman, among others.

INCREDIBLE EXPERIENCE SEEING THE TURTLE GO RIGHT UNDER AARAV'S FOOT IN GALAPAGOS

- ◆ **Get comfortable.** The first thing you need to do is make sure your children will be comfortable in the water. **The first day you go snorkeling should not be your child's first time in the water.** Instead, save it for later in your trip and use the first few days to prepare your children by swimming and floating in the pool or beach. Our son loved water but it had been a few months between trips and he had forgotten what the pool felt like. It took him a couple of hours to get comfortable in the pool again before we went snorkeling with stingrays in Grand Cayman the next day.

◆ **Find boats that allow kids.** Not all snorkeling companies will allow young children, so be sure to check for age limits and requirements when doing your research. Some will require passengers to wear wetsuits, even small children, and you may have to squeeze your children into them (not an easy task).

"Get your kids comfortable in water first."

◆ **Choose the right tour.** One type of snorkel tour will take you to one location. This is the easiest because one parent can snorkel while the other stays on board with children, and then you can swap. Another tour may be an actual tour where you have to swim and follow along with a guide. In this case, you may have to swim with your children, or, worse case, a parent stays on the boat and has to miss the tour. Be sure to ask what type of tour it will be so you are prepared, and prepare your children for what is to come.

◆ **Have the right equipment.** When we have taken our son snorkeling, we have him in a puddle jumper so he will float. There are some great seated floats that can keep young children secure, or for children more comfortable in the water puddle jumpers with arm and chest inflatables will keep your children safely above the water. We also strongly recommend you **take a life jacket or something to float with,** as well. As you snorkel with your kids, even if you are a strong swimmer, you will need to hold on to your kids, and a float will make that easier. Also, don't forget swim diapers, if your children are still in diapers or potty training.

◆ **Be prepared to take turns.** We won't try to romanticize our adventures. When we tried snorkeling along the Great Barrier Reef in Australia—our very first time attempting to snorkel with Aarav— the water was so choppy our son didn't want to go in.

When we finally cajoled him into the water in his puddle jumper, the water was so rough he was getting splashed in the face and he hated that. It was a disaster. For a situation like this, we had to take turns snorkeling. One parent stayed with our son on the boat while the other swam and then we switched places half-way through the trip.

When we were in the Galapagos, we couldn't imagine missing the opportunity to snorkel, we had heard that the underwater life there is the most amazing in the world. Our first snorkel was in Los Tuneles off the island of Isla Isabela. The waters are untouched by people except those swimming in it, so the amount of sea life is unreal. Sea turtles, sea horses, colorful fish, coral reefs— the colors are brilliant! At one point, a sea turtle swam underneath Aarav and touched his toes. Aarav had no clue what happened and the good news is that AJ captured this on a Go Pro. It was such an amazing moment and a memory to last a lifetime!

Helicopter Tours

Not all children can handle a helicopter tour, as they may be too loud and scary. **There isn't any way to know how your children will react to a helicopter ride until you actually take one.** Thankfully, most helicopter rides are very short, and even if your children are upset for 15 minutes, as ours was on our 15-minute ride over Victoria Falls, it is still worth getting that view. If you would like to try taking a helicopter tour, we learned a few things during our travels:

◆ **Be prepared for cancellations.** We have a horrible batting average with helicopter tours. We've tried to book six helicopter tours and yet only took two. Our first tour, in Hawaii, was canceled due to weather. A tour over Dubai? Canceled due to weather. So many of our trips were canceled due to weather, so be sure to have back-up plans, in case the weather doesn't cooperate when you visit a destination.

THE AWE-INSPIRING VICTORIA FALLS FROM THE HELICOPTER RIDE

◆ **Use electronics.** Helicopters are very loud, so if your children have their own headphones, such as the head covers in our travel products, take them with you. If your children need to be distracted while on the ride, give them electronics to keep them busy. (We learned the hard way not to have our offline downloads available on our iPad, so make sure you are charged and ready.) You have to sit, so you need things that will keep your children occupied and seated.

◆ **Give yourself time to settle down.** When we attempted our first helicopter ride with Aarav, many people were trying to help strap us into our seats. It was too much for him and he freaked out. Eventually, he sat on Natasha's lap and we strapped in that way, but we recommend taking the time to get settled and calm your children and not rush it.

"Helicopter rides can be hard with young kids."

◆ **Understand this may be hard.** The helicopter was one of the hardest tours we have ever done. Our son was not happy and quite upset. Not only is it loud, but they are small. We had to sit with one parent in the front and one parent in the back, and you cannot move around to help. We would even suggest, especially on a longer tour that lasts 40 minutes to an hour, splitting up and having one parent take the tour while the other stays on the ground with your child, and then switching. However, this takes a lot of time and may not be the most ideal for you.

The helicopter tour over Victoria Falls in Africa was just 15 minutes, and it is the only way to see the magnitude and scale of the falls—from the ground, you can't comprehend just how massive the falls are! As we started our ride, Aarav was not a fan of the loud noise and didn't want to get into the helicopter. We had of course come prepared to entertain him with offline videos but for some reason it didn't work on this specific ride. Natasha had to eventually hold him in her lap (buckled in) for the ride and tried to give him her phone to play some games but he wasn't having it. AJ was in the front seat and he couldn't help Natasha. Natasha is already afraid of heights and our crying child just made it worse. Unfortunately, she didn't get to see much. It was one of those scenarios where we should have switched and had AJ hold Aarav or just have taken turns going for the helicopter ride.

Safaris

We get it: Safaris can be frightening. What parent wouldn't be afraid that a lion might pounce on your vehicle and hurt your children, or that you might willingly be taking your children into areas where malaria is a serious risk? But a safari, which is only a few hours in a vehicle, can also be an incredible adventure. Where else will your children see so much wildlife in their natural habitat? **It will be single handedly the most surreal experience you will ever have.** If you have decided to invest in a safari, read on.

SO GLAD AARAV WAS SLEEPING WHEN WE SAW THE LION!

◆ **Find a child-friendly safari.** Many safaris don't allow young kids because, for good reason, it is difficult to control a small child on an actual tour. In Kruger National Park, for example, we were told it would depend on the ranger. It was too risky to book one and later discover we couldn't go. Instead, we found Chobe National Park in Botswana to be more open to taking young children and we booked that one.

"There is no more surreal experience than a safari."

◆ **Take a private safari.** When traveling with young children, we suggest avoiding a group safari because with a private tour, you can stop where you want to stop and have much more flexibility. Private tours are also more likely to accept younger children. The great thing about a private tour is you can also determine how close you get to the animals. When we saw a lion, we were lucky because our son was asleep and we knew we could be quiet enough to get close. A downside: a private safari tour can be significantly more expensive vs. similar group tours.

◆ **Understand the vehicle.** Some use covered trucks and others have you in the open. If it makes you uncomfortable to be in the open, request a closed-truck tour. That said, our guides explained the animals are used to the trucks and just see them as big objects and stay away. We rode in an open truck and felt safe, but we recommend a closed vehicle, if you can get one. Also be sure to have your children sit between the two of you, so you can control him or her.

◆ **Know safaris have food.** Safaris will be long and they include food, which is another reason they are expensive. For a private tour, they may ask you what you would like, such as milk for your children or wine for you. Before you set off, pack up the food and make sure you have all you need to be out for a few hours.

◆ **Keep quiet.** Your children need to keep more quiet when you are on safari, and you'll need to keep them settled down, especially around the animals. Bring their toy bag filled with electronics to keep them from fidgeting or getting upset if they get bored. (If possible, have your children wear headsets to keep the noise levels down.)

◆ **Don't get out of the vehicle.** These are wild animals. Do not get out of the car to take selfies. The animals will leave you alone, but don't do stupid things that will upset them or endanger you or your family. Always listen to your driver.

◆ **Take medical precautions.** If a country has malaria, you'll especially need to use bug repellent and be sure to have your medicines. Speak to your pediatrician before your trip to know what vaccinations and medications you may need before you go. We took malaria tablets before our safari and gave our son a tablet crushed into his orange juice. Then we totally doused ourselves with insect repellant.

We took a private safari to Chobe National Park in Botswana and saw some of the most amazing animals, including lions, impalas, giraffes, and hippos, all living in their natural habitat and doing their natural thing. It wasn't even 5 minutes into our first drive when we saw a herd of elephants cross right in front of our car— moms, babies, and dads came into sight and Aarav screamed "elephant!" It was amazing enough to see the herd, but it was the first time Aarav had ever said the word, and we were so excited! We also were lucky to capture that moment on video, and it quickly became one of our top moments on the entire trip.

The Best Fun Is Cheap (or Free!)

When traveling with kids, finding things to do that both children and adults will enjoy can be time consuming. The whole process of searching can make you feel anxious, especially if you don't get the just-right place to visit. The wonderful thing about traveling with young children is **they enjoy simple pleasures**. You don't need to spend a lot of money or see the biggest attraction on TripAdvisor's most-visited list. Here are some surefire winners for fun things to do when traveling with young kids.

NATASHA ENJOYING A DRINK AT THE PARK IN MALAGA

1. Neighborhood parks. A must for us, **we always find time to enjoy a park** in every city in which we travel. We begin with our accommodations by seeking Airbnbs or hotels located near parks. When we are in a new destination, we use Google Maps to find the nearest park or ask our Airbnb host for their recommendations. Having some time for our son to play and run is key for him burning energy so he may nap when we are doing the things he is less likely to enjoy. We also use parks to give each other a break. For example, AJ will take Aarav to the park while Natasha continues to get dressed in the morning, or in the afternoon to give her a break. Our favorite country for parks is Spain; they seem to have them on every block in cities like Barcelona and Madrid as well as in the smaller towns we traveled through. Often, there were parks next to bars with patios, so we could enjoy drinks and play at the same time.

AARAV ENJOYING THE PARK WITH HIS DADDY AND GRANDFATHER IN DUBAI, UAE

2. Aquariums. Children of all ages love to spend time at aquariums. One of our favorites is the Vancouver Aquarium in Stanley Park. We can enjoy aquariums together or use them as a way to split up and do some of the things we don't have a chance to do when with the kids. On a family

AARAV AND HIS COUSINS ENJOYING THE SHARKS
GO BY IN BARCELONA AQUARIUM

AARAV LEARNT ABOUT PENGIUNS AT THE CHILEAN
NATIONAL ZOO IN SANTIAGO, CHILE

trip with AJ's brother, the men took the three kids to the aquarium in Barcelona giving the ladies a chance to shop.

3. Zoos. Kids are fascinated by animals at the zoo. The small zoo in Central Park is just perfect for small kids. One of our favorites is the Zoologico Nacional in Santiago, Chile, where Natasha wanted a day to relax on our big trip around the world (it has a fantastic funicular to ride). If you don't like zoos, **you can also enjoy animals in the wild at conservation centers** such as the St. Augustine Wildlife Reserve in St. Augustine, Florida.

4. Fountains/splash pads. There is never a moment when a child doesn't want to splash and play in a fountain. Many European and South American cities are filled with fountains and splash pads such as the Circuito Magico del Agua in Lima, Peru, where Aarav had a blast chasing the water. Even if you stumble across a splash area, and you don't have the right clothing, just let them play. They'll

AARAV ENJOYING THE WATER
SPLASH PAD IN SEVILLE

have fun, and in the summer sun, dry off quickly. **Make sure you have extra diapers, however.**

AARAV AT THE MARINA BAY SANDS HOTEL IN SINGAPORE

5. Beaches or pools. Spend a day during your trip just relaxing at the pool or the beach. **Relaxing days give you a chance to unwind and connect,** and they make any kid extremely happy. We've known kids who have visited Disney parks and still remembered the hotel swimming pool more than the rides! Being at the beach also gives you a chance to hang out with the locals, and your children can play with others. Some pools are also sights worth seeing such as the Blue Lagoon in Iceland, Icebergs Pool at Bondi Beach in Sydney, and the amazing rooftop infinity pool at Marina Bay Sands hotel in Singapore where the views of the skyline are unmatched.

6. Plazas. Also popular in South America and Europe are city plazas/piazzas. When parks aren't available, pedestrian-zoned plazas can be good places to let the kids run around. **You won't have to worry about cars,** and if there are pigeons for kids to chase, even better (our son can't get enough of pigeons!). In Florence, we found a carousel in the Piazza della Repubblica to ride as well.

AARAV PLAYING WITH THE BIRDS IN SALTA, ARGENTINA

7. Street fairs/markets. Street fairs are great because they give you a sense of the local arts and crafts and often have fun things like children's areas, carousels, and live music. Whether you plan ahead and seek out special events or you stumble across a fair, they can be a blast. Aarav loved the live music at a street fair in Asheville, spending 30 minutes mesmerized by the band. In Marseille, he enjoyed the carousel at a street market, and even though Pike Place Market is a food market, he loved seeing all the fish in Seattle.

8. Ferries/boat rides. This is our fourth suggestion that involves water and we can't stress this enough: kids love water! **You don't need to take expensive water tours, simply hop on a ferry** and just be on the water, taking in the skyline. Aarav loved watching the water when we took the

AARAV SPENT AN HOUR WATCHING THIS BAND PLAY AT THE ASHEVILLE STREET FAIR IN NORTH CAROLINA

AARAV WATCHING THE WATER FROM THE FERRY FROM VENICE TO MURANO

ferry from Venice to Murano and enjoyed running on the boat while we enjoyed seeing the amazing night lights in cities like Budapest, Shanghai, and Hong Kong.

9. Unique museums. Not all museums are stuffy art museums that will bore the kids. **Many museums can both be entertaining for adults and a blast for the kids.** Look for museums offering children's programs, scavenger hunts, and crafts, well as unique museums featuring things your kids love. A couple of our favorites are the Miniatur Wunderland Museum in Hamburg (the most unique museum we have ever seen) and the Car and Fashion Museum in Malaga, Spain.

AARAV AT THE CAR AND FASHION MUSEUM IN MALAGA

10. Malls. Yes, we have malls on the list. They are great for rainy days when you are stuck indoors, or to just get a chance to shop, as **most malls around the world have play areas for kids.** In Singapore, for example, we found a kids' area Aarav could play, run around, and go down slides while Natasha went shopping.

AARAV IN THE PLAY AREA IN SINGAPORE COMING DOWN A SLIDE

Did you notice that none of the suggestions on this list are expensive attractions? It's easier to find fun things to do without having to spend a ton, and you'll still get to **immerse your family in a new places and cultures.**

The More, The Merrier

When we tell our story about traveling around the world with our two-year-old son, people are amazed, although there are parents who wonder just how much of our advice works for parents of multiple kids. While we have only one child, we did, in fact, travel with multiple children when we traveled with our extended family, which we often did. While there are some changes that come with more children, **many of the things we learned carry over to larger families.**

Traveling with more than one child means using slightly different seat-booking strategies, needing more space, managing multiple kids running in different directions, having more mouths to feed (and hunger issues), and entertaining several ages.

Our family and friends traveling with us played a huge part in the development of this book, and we have turned to them for advice on traveling with multiple kids.

Packing tips

Get a double stroller. A double stroller is a necessity when you travel with two kids who will likely need to be in the stroller at the same time. A good travel double stroller is the Zoe XL2 Double Stroller. Of course, you won't be able to take a double stroller on the plane as you can with our recommended single stroller, the GB Pockit. If you really need a stroller in the airport (and don't want to check a double stroller at the gate), consider some of the other options below.

Buy an add-on to your stroller. With more children comes a need for a larger stroller. Skip the double stroller that sits two children across, as the wide berth will be difficult for narrow spaces and easy travel. Instead, try front/back systems, and, if traveling with slightly older children who can walk but may get tired, consider an add-on such as the BuggyBoard Saddle. The saddle attaches to most strollers. This works well for children who have a few years between their ages.

Use a baby carrier and stroller combination. To help minimize space, using a baby carrier or backpack can allow one parent to carry a child while the other uses a smaller one-child stroller—a simple solution that is easier to navigate with than a double stroller. Using this strategy, when the older child gets tired, you can allow them to ride in the stroller and carry the younger one in the carrier. If both kids are small, you can swap who sits in the stroller and who sits in the carrier. A basic carrier that works well and does not cost a fortune is the Infantino Flip 4-in-1 Convertible Carrier.

Pack toys your kids won't fight over. If your children fight over certain toys, make your life easier by not bringing the toys that will cause a scene. If the toy is essential, bring the same toys for all kids, so they can't fight over a sibling having something they want.

Pack easily shared toys. In tight spaces, playtime may only be available in the space in front of your kids—like a table at a restaurant or the tray table on an airplane. Packing small items they can play with together, such as Play-Doh or watercolor books (just add water and the picture comes to life), can be entertaining with easy cleanup.

Tips for flying on a plane

Book your seats in advance. With more than three people, traveling becomes trickier in terms of how you will sit together, especially when planes offer only two or three seats together. The cheapest flights rarely allow one to select seats, but to guarantee you aren't separating the family or having to scramble as you board to find someone to swap seats with, book your seats when you book your flight.

Seating strategy. With most airline seating only offering two or three seats together, determine how your family will configure a seating arrangement. Some families will reserve seats in the same row on opposite sides of the aisle, while others will sit in similar seats in front/back of each other. Sometimes, parents prefer to take the aisle seats, effectively locking in their children. Remember, in *Buckle Up Fast With Your Boarding Pass*, we discussed how implementing our Plane Seat Hacking Strategy with only one child can help you gain up to $1,077 worth of free space over three-year period. With two or three children, you can double or even triple the value you're getting! Take a look at our recommendations here, and give it a try!

Some configurations you can try for two kids include:

1. Two aisle seats beside two middle seats
2. Two seats in one row and the exact same two seats the row behind
3. A window and an aisle seat, in hopes of securing an empty space between you for extra room, and the exact seats the row behind

To see configurations for both two and three kids, see the following graphic.

THE 2 IDIOTS PLANE SEAT HACKING STRATEGY - 2 CHILDREN

2 CHILDREN/2-SEAT CONFIGURATION

OR

2 CHILDREN/3-SEAT CONFIGURATION

OR

2 CHILDREN/4-SEAT CONFIGURATION

THE 2 IDIOTS PLANE SEAT
HACKING STRATEGY - 3 CHILDREN

3 CHILDREN/2-SEAT CONFIGURATION

3 CHILDREN/3-SEAT CONFIGURATION

OR

3 CHILDREN/4-SEAT CONFIGURATION

OR

Eating on the plane. It's much harder to manage feeding your kids when there is more than one. Serve your children first, and then have the flight attendant bring your food after the kids are done. If meals do not come with your flight, and you must purchase them, you should purchase your meal in advance, or when the attendants come by, so they do not sell out before you get to eat.

Use credit cards with lounge access. Enroll in credit cards that have lounge rewards because it can really add up when you have multiple kids. For example, in the United States, the Chase Sapphire Reserve card gives you free access to airport lounges in several countries and provides free food and drinks, quiet spaces, and sometimes showers.

Handling the kids

Share responsibility. When one of your kids gets extra fussy, which will happen, make a point of tending to the child who is the worst, because the other kids will follow suit. Share the load, so to speak, and don't have one parent do all of the calming. Give each other breaks from tending to the kids, so you don't end up getting too fussy yourself.

Give kids responsibility. Ask your older children to help out. This not only gives you a hand but teaches them responsibility and gives them a task to do. Older kids like to help keep the little ones in place, whether it is sitting next to them at a restaurant or watching them at a playground. Allow your children (if old enough) to be in charge of their own bags. They may struggle at first, but as they learn, travel will become much easier in the long run.

In summary, **don't shy away from traveling with kids.** The challenges you experience make you stronger as a family and you will return home with great memories. No matter how many children you travel with, combining these tips will always lead to a rewarding trip.

Our Favorites

We get asked this question frequently. What were your favorite places? What are your favorite apps? What are your favorite websites? etc. Those can be hard questions to answer because favorite things really depend on what you are looking for and every country, every city, every toy—really every human—offers something special and unique. Regardless, we have attempted to compile our list of favorites.

We hope this can give you a headstart in planning travel for your family!

Don't forget to also visit our resources page at www.the2idiots.com/resources/ for all the links in this section - kid-friendly itineraries for our recommended destinations, recommended products, sites and apps!

. . . .

Destinations For Every Occasion

Top 3 countries for travel with kids
◆ **Spain, Peru, Singapore**

> Having traveled around the world with our son, we were quick to discover the countries and cities most welcoming to children. Spain is our absolute No. 1 country, with Peru and Singapore both a close second. There are literally parks on every corner, kids are welcome everywhere, and being together as a family is a big part of the lifestyle even later into the night. In Singapore, one steps off a

plane and immediately sees how kid-friendly the country is: there are actually child-sized potties inside the airport.

Top 3 beach destinations

◆ **Indonesia (Bali), United Arab Emirates (Dubai), Bahamas (Eleuthera)**

Beach destinations have to have calm waters and stunning beaches, of course. But for us, we also like beach destinations that offer culture and things to see when we aren't lounging by the sea. Bali is a great example because it has so much to see and do in addition to its beaches. Visiting temples, enjoying great food and great snorkeling experiences—all with extremely budget-friendly rates— make Bali a top destination! In Dubai, you get to rest and relax plus enjoy the incredible energy of this thriving city. And, for the most pristine beaches we have ever seen, Eleuthera in the Outer Islands of the Bahamas tops our list.

Top 3 countries for food

◆ **China, Spain, India (slight bias)**

We like countries that can offer us incredible diversity in foods with multiple regions offering different styles of cooking. China surprised us the most because it was the best food experience we had on our big trip. Each region has a different type of food, from Turkish-like flavors in western China to curries in southwestern China to the soup dumplings, hotpot, and seafood dishes along the eastern coast—it's all incredible. In Spain, we love that the people make eating an experience, plus the ability to sample so many foods during a meal by ordering tapas. And yes, we are slightly biased when it comes to Indian food. But again, the country has so many different areas with different styles of food, all of which are incredibly flavorful. Yum!

Top 3 cities for food

◆ **Cape Town, New York, Shanghai**

Our need for diversity in our dining continues into cities. There are just certain cities that experiment with foods from around the world. Filled with neighborhoods with people from around the world bringing their culture's favorite dishes to a new place means we get to sample more cultures and foods in one place. In New York, Shanghai, and Cape Town, you can find Italian, Greek, Indian, Turkish, French, Chinese, Ethiopian and more! Each are truly cosmopolitan cities with so much to offer.

Top 3 incredible cities
◆ **Shanghai, Vancouver, Dubai**

When we think of an incredible city, we think of energy and spirit that comes experiencing strong growth, great diversity in people, world-class cuisine, awesome sightseeing, and great shopping. Shanghai, Vancouver, and Dubai have all of these things in spades! These are places that have so much to offer not only to tourists but also its residents. We enjoyed them so much we could see ourselves living in any one of these three cities.

Top 3 most unexpectedly awesome cities
◆ **Tallinn (Estonia), Cape Town (South Africa), Zagreb (Croatia)**

When you plan trips to certain cities, it is because you have heard great things and have high expectations. Other times, you stumble upon cities that you never realized would be so awesome. Cape Town has great diversity of people and cultures due to its geographical location, plus you get to enjoy the incredible sights and sounds of the entire Cape Peninsula. And both Zagreb and Tallinn are up-and-coming cities with young, growing democracies that offer lots of energy.

Top 3 countries for history
◆ **China, Peru, Italy**

AJ is the one who especially wants to uncover history on our adventures, but we were both wowed by China, Peru, and Italy. Thousands of years of history tell the story of how these countries, and the world, have evolved over time as seen through museums, architecture, and artifacts. In China, think about the Shang Dynasty that dates back to 1600 B.C. There are written records from these ancient people who built what is now modern China. In Peru, places like Pachacamac outside of Lima teaches us about the rise and fall of the Inca civilization. And finally, Italy's history is embedded in Western Civilization, with the Roman Empire affecting Europe, Africa, the Middle East, and Asia. To us, these are must-see countries.

Top 3 nature and beauty destinations
◆ **Iceland, Patagonia, Alaska**

Sometimes travel can show you places and people you would never have encountered at home. Sometimes travel can show you such beauty that you'll never be able to clear your memory of it. We have traveled to places with incredible beauty, but Iceland was just breathtaking and #1 on our rankings of Top nature and beauty destinations. Filled with geysers, rocks shooting out of the oceans, glaciers, and hot springs... it's just so unique and offers a setting we may not see anywhere else in world. Patagonia and Alaska are also similar in providing some of the last remaining untouched lands in the world.

Top 3 wildlife destinations
◆ **Tanzania, Galapagos, Botswana**

There is something humbling about seeing animals still occupying nature, living life without human interaction. Of course, children also adore animals. Instead of seeing animals held captive in the zoo, visiting them in their natural environments can provide wonderful memories. In the Galapagos, we found some of the best underwater life we've ever seen while snorkeling and diving. In the African nations of Botswana and Tanzania, taking a safari and seeing a lion just a few feet away or a herd of elephants making their way to a watering hole is a surreal experience.

Top 3 human-made wonders
◆ **Hoover Dam (Nevada), Panama Canal (Panama City), Burj Khalifa (Dubai)**

When you stand before the Hoover Dam, the Panama Canal or the world's tallest building of Burj Khalifa, you cannot help but say "Wow!" It's hard to comprehend how man could create these wonders. The creativity and how the mind works, especially to create solutions to help people, is fascinating. The Hoover Dam powers multiple states with its water, while the Panama Canal shaved months off of travel by creating a cut-through between the Atlantic and Pacific Oceans. In Dubai, the Burj Khalifa is a symbol of how fast the city is growing; a symbol of man's achievements. Again, "Wow!"

Top 3 natural wonders
◆ **Victoria Falls (Zimbabwe), Grand Canyon (Arizona), Natural Geysers (Iceland)**

How can anyone visit one of the world's natural wonders and not be in awe? It's nearly impossible to look at the Grand Canyon and not be stunned by the amazing monument that has been carved out of water over millions of years. The size, scale, and scope of Victoria Falls in Africa are difficult to put into words. It is simply the most incredible waterfall we have ever seen. And in Iceland, geyser is actually an Icelandic word that means "to rush." Watching geysers shoot off into the sky where the word was invented is quite a moment.

Top 3 Instagram-worthy destinations
◆ **Greek Isles (Santorini, Mykonos), Italy (Amalfi coast), Iceland**

These days, travel is also about capturing the perfect shot. For the most stunning back drops to your family photo, the best pictures will be taken on the Greek Isles of Santorini and Mykonos, where your colorful clothes can pop off white-washed homes and cliffside views of the Adriatic Sea; along further cliffs with dramatic views along Italy's Amalfi Coast; and, again, against the stunning beauty that makes up the entire island of Iceland.

Top 3 cruises we've taken
◆ **Mediterranean Cruise (Princess), Alaska Cruise (Norwegian), Scandinavia Cruise (Norwegian)**

We love cruising and have taken several cruises in different areas of the world. We prefer cruises with a great mix of things to see over the party cruises that go to the Caribbean. We want to see amazing ports of call and use a cruise ship to get us to multiple destinations, while also providing some family fun onboard. The Mediterranean cruises offer amazing itineraries where in one sailing you can experience different countries and cultures. The Alaskan cruises will showcase wildlife, glaciers, and beautiful scenery. And on a cruise in Scandinavia, you get a combination of both.

Sites To Check Before You Jet

Book single-destination flights: Kayak

Explore flights to multiple destinations: Google Flights

Book hotels: Kayak

Book Airbnb: Airbnb

Plan your travel: TripAdvisor

Best app to translate language: Google Translate

Store digital offline copies of your important files: Dropbox

International vaccination travel center (USA Only): Passport Health Center

Have No Fear - Grab The Right Gear

Travel Stroller (children over 6 months) - gb Pockit: lightweight stroller with easy folding mechanism and serious carrying capacity.

Travel Car Seat (children over 22 pounds) - IMMI GO: portable, lightweight, easy to install, and it comes with an attached carrying case. It's also easy to store and fits in the overhead bin of your flight!

Flying Harness (1+ years, over 22 pounds) - CARES Airplane Safety Harness: designed specifically for plane travel, this harness is easy to install and helps keep your small child safer on a plane.

Travel Crib - Guava Family Lotus Travel Crib: very portable and small enough to be a carry-on, this travel crib takes 15 seconds to set up.

Credit Card (USA only) - Chase Sapphire Reserve: this card gives you 50 percent more points when you use it for travel-related expenses, and Priority Pass gives you access to certain airport lounges.

Travel Cell Phone Provider (USA only) - T-Mobile: with unlimited data, texts, and calls AND with unlimited data in over 140 countries, T-Mobile makes it significantly easier to travel.

Don't Leave Home Without These Apps

YouTube Premium: we subscribe to YouTube Premium only when we are traveling so we can download all of our son's favorite educational shows.

Kindle Fire Kids Edition: ton of great apps and videos that you can download straight to the Kindle. Be aware of the drawback that the downloads only last 48 hours before having to reconnect to the internet.

ChuChu TV: a subscription-based app where you can access a great library of videos for your kids. Videos are educational with super-diverse characters. These videos can be downloaded to any smart device.

The Monkey Preschool Series: a bundle of apps, which you can download a la carte or as a group, that are designed to fit your child's current skill level.

Baby Flashcards Apps: available in different languages—we have the Hindi and English—it lets your child build a robust vocabulary. Our son finds this app to be completely engrossing!

Smart Baby Apps: great set of apps that allow your child to learn alphabets and words, match shapes and colors, learn to sort, and develop some puzzle-solving skills (Smart Baby ABC, Smart Shapes, Smart Baby Touch, Smart Sorter).

Funny Foods Learning Games: not so much an app as an entire library of mini-apps and games, this is an endlessly appealing way for kids to learn.

Dr. Seuss ABCs: our son loves this app and it has helped him learn his alphabet.

Netflix: Doesn't have too many great options for kids, but now that Netflix offers downloadable video options, we use it while traveling.

Gifts That Make Travel Easier

The Look What I Made Govinci Suitcase has a drawing board right on the outside so your child can color and stay occupied.

The Trunki Suitcase gives kids a ride while they travel.

The Chibiya Panda Travel Neck Pillow doubles as a hoodie.

PopYum Baby Bottle is a must-have for traveling with young children. Store formula in the cap of the bottle and a push of a button drops the powder into the water for no-mess mixing and measuring.

CozyPhones are comfortable fabric headbands with built-in removable headphones. They stay on, don't tangle, and keep kids warm.

Not Parent Approved Card Game will keep older kids and teens (and parents) entertained.

Getting comfortable on long flights just got a little easier with the **FlyPal inflatable footrest**. Deflated, easily fits into your carry-on for inflating and flexible use onboard. Use the smaller cushion as a travel pillow.

BuddyBagzs serve as a pillow and bed, all in one. It can be used as a backpack for an easy carry-all.

Small enough to carry in a purse, the **Cozy Cover Easy Seat High Chair** can fit all chairs and gives you a high chair everywhere you go.

The new **Fire HD 8 Kids Edition Tablet** helps when nothing else will. This is our favorite gadget for our son.

Adios, Sayonara, Goodbye...For Now

Thank you so much for joining our travel family and taking the first step toward traveling more with your children. We will continue to work hard to make travel with your little one easier!

Remember to always **Be F.L.E.X.I.B.L.E.** Also, don't forget to visit our blog at www.2idiotstravel.com or follow us on social media (see handles below) where we will continue to provide ideal itineraries and kid-friendly advice for the 100+ destinations we have visited. We will continue posting articles on our blog.

Here are some examples:

Why it's Easier to Travel with Kids Than Ever Before
What We Learned on Our Sabbatical (And What it Means for Your Vacation)
7 Tips on Surviving a Walking Tour with Your Child
How Do You Pack for an 8.5-Month Trip Across the World?
Protecting Your Memories

How We Prioritize Travel in our Finances
Communication in Non-English Speaking Countries
Step-By-Step on Finding the Best Private Transportation in a City
Planning the Perfect Itinerary at a Destination
And much more ...

We would also love to hear how this book helped you in your family travels. Please tag us with #2idiotstravel and #howtotravelwithkids on social media so we can keep in touch. Who knows, you may just be featured in an upcoming article or post!

We also want to give you an exclusive invite to the Family Travel Network, our community for families that travel with young children. Connect with other parents that have bought the book, ask any questions and learn from their experiences. Please go to www.facebook.com/groups/familytravelnetwork/ to join.

Finally, don't forget to visit our resources page at www.the2idiots.com/resources/ for a free digital download of this book, plus a comprehensive list of links to our referenced articles, recommended products, downloadable checklists and more for all of your travel needs!

If there is something specific you would like us to write about or have a question, please contact us on hello@2idiotstravel.com.

There are plenty of reasons to not travel; we think the reasons to travel are more compelling. Why wait? Travel now!

#2idiotstravel #howtotravelwithkids

Follow-us on social media

www.instagram.com/2idiotstravel   www.facebook.com/2idiotstravel
www.twitter.com/2idiotstravel   www.pinterest.com/2idiotstravel
            www.youtube.com/2idiotstravel

Acknowledgements

Without our son Aarav and his ability to find joy and show flexibility in any situation, we wouldn't have these amazing, lifelong memories to share—and there would be no book! Thank you, Aarav, for your sense of adventure and ability to make every new experience unforgettable.

We would like to give a huge thank-you to our loving and supportive parents, Jaiprakash and Jayshree Ratani and Ashima Sandhir and the late Satish Sandhir. They not only encouraged our drive for success, but they also fostered our love for and ability to travel. They instilled in us the joy of leaving home and exploring the world.

We would also like to thank Amanda Clark and Lissa Poirot, who wrote many articles that culminated in the vision of the book, and our friend Priti Damle, who provided the inspiration for our name, "The 2 Idiots."

To our designers—Katie Halter, who designed our amazing interior and incorporated endless edits to get to this point; and Elena Reznikova, who not only designed this beautiful cover but didn't give up until it was perfected—thank you for sharing your amazing talents and helping to bring this book to fruition.

To our editors: Chandi Lyn Broadbent, who provided our initial edit; Lora Sickora, who performed our final edits and helped get our book to this incredible point; Julia Bramer, who brought this book to life on digital devices; Jennifer Weers, who helped build an amazing index inspite of our last-minute notice—thank you all for your hard work and understanding our voice and mission to help other parents experience the thrill of travel.

We would also like to thank our friends, Nadia Morales and Nithya Pulimood, who provided feedback on our book—especially on the chapter The More, The Merrier. We value your experience and your friendship. Thank you for providing so much valuable input.

Finally, thank you to our brother and sister-in-law, Atirek and Ashley Ratani, who've joined us on many journeys, taught us many travel lessons, and provided extremely helpful feedback. We appreciate you so much. This book would not be the same without your input.

Always with you in travel,

Natasha, AJ and Aarav

Index

Printed in Great Britain
by Amazon

72892612R00108